Chapter By Chapter

Emily Zondlak

Chapbook Press

Schuler Books
2660 28th Street SE
Grand Rapids, MI 49512
(616) 942-7330
www.schulerbooks.com

ISBN 13: 9781943359851

eBook ISBN: 9781943359868

Library of Congress Control Number: 2017958940

Copyright © 2017 Emily Zondlak
All rights reserved.

No part of this book may be reproduced in any form without express permission of the copyright holder.

Printed in the United States by Chapbook Press.

Chapter By Chapter

Chapter By Chapter

Saved?

All Scripture God-breathed and is useful for teaching, rebuking, correcting and training in righteousness, so that the servant of God may be thoroughly equipped for every good work. (2 Timothy 3:16-17) In life, there's a constant struggle or battle of you behaving in such as a way that one, you act how you want to, or two, you try to and live according to what is pleasing to Lord God Almighty, the Maker of the Heavens and earth. Strive to illuminate 2 Timothy 2:15 in your life: "Do your best to present yourself to God as one approved, a worker who does not need to be ashamed and who correctly handles the word of truth."

You may be questioning the meaning behind being "born again" into Christ Jesus or Jesus Christ. First of all, Christ Jesus and Jesus Christ mean the same Person. He is a triune being, which means that He is three Persons in one: God the Father, Christ the Son, and the Holy Spirit.

So, back to your question of the meaning behind being "born again" into Christ Jesus or Jesus Christ. Romans 10:9 states, "If you declare with your mouth, "Jesus is Lord," and believe in your heart that God raised him from the dead, you will be saved." When someone is of age to understand right from wrong, such as a five-year-old, he or she can be saved and make the decision to be born again. It does not matter if you are five-years-old or 195; just believe without having the slightest doubt in your heart, confess with your lips that Jesus is Lord you shall be saved!

How do you get saved? First of all, Jesus is the **<u>only</u>** **<u>Name</u>** by which you can be saved. (Acts 4:12) Jesus is The Way to get to God and enter eternal life, in which states in John 14:6. You will be persecuted for your faith and love for Jesus in this life, but stand firm in Christ because one day very soon, your eyes will see the Lord's glory!

John 3:16 is a fairly known Scripture verse so say it with me. "For God so loved the world that he gave his one and only Son, that whoever believes in him shall not perish but have eternal life." You need to confess in the Name of Jesus. When you do and make this life-long journey decision, you and Him are co-partners in life. Daily reading the Word of God (Bible) and praying; having conversations with your Almighty Father (God) are keys in order to understand Him, believe in Him, and trust Him.

You may be questioning what "believe" really means. It's when you make the decision to stop living the way that you want to and totally rely on God to lead, guide, and provide for you in life through the power of His Holy Spirit. The parable of Matthew 19:16-22 depicts the important decision to make Jesus Christ to be your personal Lord and Savior. Afterwards, I'll explain the parable from my own life story.

(Matthew 19:16-22) "A man approached him and said, "Teacher, what good thing must I do to have eternal life?" Jesus said, "Why do you ask me about what is good? There's only one who is good. If you want to enter eternal life, keep the commandments." The man said, "Which ones?" Then Jesus said, "Don't commit murder. Don't commit adultery. Don't steal. Don't give false testimony. Honor your father and mother, and love your neighbor as you love yourself." The young man replied, "I've kept all these. What am I still missing?" Jesus said, "If you want to be complete, go, sell what you own, and give the money to the poor. Then you will have treasure in heaven. And come follow me." But when the young man heard this, he went away saddened, because he had many possessions." Many people don't want to give up their possessions because they think that it's what satisfies them because of the messages of the world, such as fancy cars, name-brand clothes, and etc. Once people achieve these dreams, if they are honest, these dreams don't satisfy them.

Luke 15:11–32 states, "Jesus continued: "There was a man who had two sons. The younger one said to his father, 'Father, give me my share of the estate.' So he divided his property between them.

"Not long after that, the younger son got together all he had, set off for a distant country and there squandered his wealth in wild living. After he had spent everything, there was a severe famine in that whole country, and he began to be in need. So he went and hired himself out to a citizen of that country, who sent him to his fields to feed pigs. He longed to fill his stomach with the pods that the pigs were eating, but no one gave him anything.

"When he came to his senses, he said, 'How many of my father's hired servants have food to spare, and here I am starving to death! I will set out and go back to my father and say to him: Father, I have sinned against heaven and against you. I am no longer worthy to be called your son; make me like one of your hired servants.' So he got up and went to his father.

"But while he was still a long way off, his father saw him and was filled with compassion for him; he ran to his son, threw his arms around him and kissed him.

"The son said to him, 'Father, I have sinned against heaven and against you. I am no longer worthy to be called your son.'

"But the father said to his servants, 'Quick! Bring the best robe and put it on him. Put a ring on his finger and sandals on his feet. Bring the fattened calf and kill it. Let's have a feast and celebrate. For this son of mine was dead and is alive again; he was lost and is found.' So they began to celebrate.

"Meanwhile, the older son was in the field. When he came near the house, he heard music and dancing. So he called one of the servants and asked him what was going on. 'Your brother has come,' he replied, 'and your father has killed the fattened calf because he has him back safe and sound.'

Chapter By Chapter

"The older brother became angry and refused to go in. So his father went out and pleaded with him. But he answered his father, 'Look! All these years I've been slaving for you and never disobeyed your orders. Yet you never gave me even a young goat so I could celebrate with my friends. But when this son of yours who has squandered your property with prostitutes comes home, you kill the fattened calf for him!'

"'My son,' the father said, 'you are always with me, and everything I have is yours. But we had to celebrate and be glad, because this brother of yours was dead and is alive again; he was lost and is found.'"

I have the physical disability called Cerebral Palsy and am nonverbal. When I was born, my mom's uterus ruptured and the doctors had to perform an emergency C-Section. My mom's and my life were in danger and the doctors did not know if my mom or I would live. As you can see, we lived! I was without oxygen for three to seven minutes so that was what caused me to have Cerebral Palsy; the lack of oxygen my brain wasn't receiving.

During my childhood, I participated in downhill skiing with my family, Little League T-Ball and hip-hop dance classes to be active. Seasons in my life through these activities, I was just trying to fill a need to be accepted for the person I was. Of course, these activities did not erase that empty feeling in my heart. I was trying to live up to the worldviews of being happy.

Chapter By Chapter

God led me to a youth group called Access, and it sounded interesting. I joined for all of the wrong reasons. It was something I could attend during the summer and was in my age group of people. The first few months I was about having friends because I had the world's mindset. I typed up a little blurb about my hopes, interests, and how my university online worked. When someone started speaking to me and couldn't understand me, I handed he or she this piece of paper. Attending this youth group and hearing that when God is in your life, you will be changed. You will live life differently. Often I thought it would not be true and that this was crazy. I watched criminal TV shows, watched chick-flick and romance movies, and enjoyed listening to country music. So I thought that I wouldn't change my interests, hobbies, or anything else for that matter.

All of us sin and we try not to, but God is still working on us. Some of people's sins are addictions such as, alcohol or sex. I had a bad addiction when I was at the age of where my body was changing and had weird feelings. I didn't know how to handle this new change. I grew up in the period when instant messengering in chat rooms was a fad. My parents trusted me and gave me a computer. It has my adapted tools to successfully use it. I bet that you are asking yourself what kind of addiction did she have? Even the disabled can have addictions. I am not so innocent as some of you may think I am because of my disability. Well my computer helped and helps me to have a social life. It takes away my speech barrier and the judging barrier. My addiction was Internet sex with no cameras or pictures thankfully. I didn't go that far. I don't remember how long this lasted but I hid it. Something inside of me knew it was wrong of me to be doing this because I cleared my Internet history after I was finished to avoid getting in trouble. I don't remember how I quit because I looked forward to doing this addiction. Thankfully I stopped.

In October of 2009 I gave my life fully to God. I hit my rock bottom and God became real. God was not distant and I did not have to complete rituals or sacraments for God to love me. Religion kills the soul, but relationship with the Holy Sprit brings life when you are intimate with God; speaking to Him about your daily life. I said, "Goodbye" to religion and going through the motions in my parents' church as well as friends' faith. I was being a pew warmer believer. When I decided to have an intimate relationship with God, I cried. Jesus lifted my burdens off from me. I felt as though God breathed His breath of life in me. He flipped His light in me, so darkness fled from me. God's rivers of living water were as though I was driving my wheelchair on them as I moved. My fears were gone. I felt as though Jesus' light was beaming in me; smiling from ear to ear. I had unspeakable joy!

Just like the Matthew 19:16-22 and Luke 15:11–32 parables, you too can be alive and on fire for Lord Jesus Christ! God is waiting for you with arms wide open to take care of you. All you have to do is to walk away from your messed up life, whether that is consumed with pornography, drugs, alcohol, partying, gambling addictions, or rage, etc. and desire God to make you the person that He created you to be. Read Romans 5 and 6 about how Jesus Christ loves you so incredibly much that He died on the cross for you to give life! All I want is for you to know God personally, intimately, and live life that glorifies Him! When you believe in Jesus Christ, it's **the most important** and **the best** decision that you will **ever** make in your life! Choose Jesus Christ to be your personal Lord and Savior of your life!

Chapter By Chapter

Holy Spirit

If you are just "born again" and made Jesus Christ to be your personal Lord and Savior of your life, CONGRATULATIONS! Welcome to God's family! You are Christ's son or daughter! Tell fellow believers in Christ Jesus your decision to follow Jesus, Holy Spirit in life as well as you are choosing Jesus to be your personal Lord and Savior of your life. They will be ecstatic and will rejoice with you. Also telling fellow believers in Lord Jesus Christ is a word of truth and is found in 1 Timothy 6:12. Now you have to be filled with the Holy Spirit or in other words, be Spirit-filled.

God and Jesus is sitting on His throne in the Heavens above all Heavens; Jesus Christ is sitting at the right-hand-side of God. I like to acknowledge God as Father God or Father Almighty because I am honored to call Him <u>my</u> Father and am so in love with Him that I'm proud to call Him Father God and Father Almighty! So in this book I tend to say Father God and Father Almighty instead of God; just know that I'm referring to God because there's <u>only one true God!</u> So God and Jesus is sitting His throne in the Heavens above all Heavens and the Holy Spirit is on the earth reporting back to God about what is happening on earth. Holy Spirit is in all ways God so He, God is everywhere!

Holy Spirit is the power source of the triune God [Father, Son, and Holy Spirit]. (Luke 24:49 & Acts 1:8) His jobs are to lead, guide, provide for you, and teach you God's ways as well as the things to come. (John 16:13-15) In John 14:15-27 explains His jobs.

You need to ask Father God for His promised gift of Holy Spirit. Just pray to God for Holy Spirit, but don't have the smallest or the teeny-tiniest bit of doubt in your heart when you are asking for His Holy Spirit. In Luke 11:13, Jesus says, "If you then, though you are evil, know how to give good gifts to your children, how much more will your Father in heaven give the Holy Spirit to those who ask him!" You just have to ask Father God!

John Bevere with Addison Bevere have a book entitled *The Holy Spirit: An Introduction Book* in which, they explain God's Holy Spirit in-depth. I strongly urge and encourage in reading their book to better understand whom God, Holy Spirit is! The DVD sessions are word-for-word what the book has printed on its' pages. So if you don't enjoy reading a lot, check out John Bevere with Addison Bevere' DVD sessions!

Holy Spirit is the Helper, in which He teaches you the awesome and incredible mysteries of God! In John 14:26, Jesus says, "But the Helper, the Holy Spirit, whom the Father will send in my name, will teach you all things and remind you of everything that I have told you." He won't do everything for you. Think of Him as your coach and teammate; you have to complete your part and vice versa, in which Holy Spirit will do

His part in your relationship. You are building an intimate relationship with Him so the quality time; you spend reading God's Word (Bible), praying to Father God, and practicing or applying His Word to your life, the more you will be like Christ and known by God! (1 Corinthians 8:3)

It has been said that the Word of God (Bible) is difficult to understand as well as boring. If you have this opinion, you need to pray to God for His Holy Spirit because God, His Word is alive and active. (Hebrews 4:12) The more quality time you spend with God desiring to know Him intimately, the more God will reveal Himself to you! (John 14:21)

In this book, through God's leading and guiding by His Holy Spirit, He has outlined just the New Testament of His Word with encouragements to strengthen your faith in Jesus Christ as well as your love relationship for Him; challenging you to live life that is holy, blameless, and pleasing to God, your Father. The chapters of the New Testament are depicted going from chapter by chapter to help you better understand God and how to practice applying His Word to your life to impact His kingdom!

The Old Testament books' chapters are not included in this book because it explains laws and traditions of how Father God wanted people to live before He sent His Son Jesus to live on earth, to serve people, to die on the cross, and to be raised to life for everyone to have salvation [eternal life] through

Him! Father God desires His children to love and have compassion for Him first, then others. Illuminate Christ's forgiveness and help in positive ways, especially in the difficult times. Stop going through the motions of trying to act faithful to God when God's zeal [great energy or enthusiasm in pursuit of Him] is not in your heart! The Old Testament or old covenant explains the law, commandments, statutes and judgments, in which God laid down for people to obey. The old covenant involved people relying on themselves or being self-determined. Even though they committed themselves to obeying God, they didn't want to take responsibly of living life pleasing to Him. They chose to live life that went against God's laws.

    The old covenant had flaws because of people's actions. Everything (the law, commandments, statutes and judgments) considering the old covenant was flawless, but the people were not flawless. It has been said that the law of the old covenant represents God; holy, just, and good. So the old covenant does not become erase because of Jesus Christ's death and resurrection. It helps people understand what to do and what not to do. When you have faith in God and obey His commands with a complete sincerity and commitment in your heart, you illuminate the faith and love God desires His children to have within them.

So the new covenant or the New Testament is established through Jesus Christ's death and resurrection. Faith in Jesus Christ is the better covenant because the promises are better, such as the Holy Spirit and Jesus addresses the fault with the old covenant! Jesus Christ's death and resurrection, Jesus made a way and makes it possible for your sins not to be remembered if you have sincerity in your heart and stop, turn a 180-degree turn from your sin, walking away from it. He forgives you, your sins and remembers them no longer. (Hebrews 8:12) Jesus came to earth and lived in human likeness for about 33 years; He knows and understands the stresses of life bring (Hebrews 4:15) so you can pray to God about your feelings and thoughts about your current life season. This is an attribute of the better promises of the new covenant. The old covenant kept people at a distance and a mediator [a person made the people's sins become amended or cleared of their sin, wrong] spoke on their behalf to Father God. Since Jesus Christ's death and resurrection, a mediator is not needed and God desires you to approach His throne in boldness and confidence. (Ephesians 3:12 & Hebrews 4:16) But approach God's throne in reverential fear [deep respect] of Him and with humility!

    The new covenant, God puts His laws and Word in your mind and on your heart through His power of His Holy Spirit to teach and remind you of how to live life glorifying Him. He desires a close intimate relationship with you! Enjoy building and deepening a strong, firm, as well as intimate relationship with God the [your] Father, Christ the Son, and Holy Spirit! As Jesus says in John 16:33, "In this world you will have trouble. Insert trouble as tribulation and it means [a cause of great trouble or suffering] But take heart! I have overcome the world." Jesus warns us, His children that life on earth, while He is seated in the Heavens above all Heaven will not be easy. He makes a way possible for us to be completely satisfied. To be completely satisfied in life is by knowing who God is, understanding Jesus, and trusting in His Holy Spirit!

Matthew

Chapter 1 We are connected or related to one another because of Jesus Christ. We should love and bless others just as God our Father and Jesus Christ loves. We are scared of the unknown, but if you love and trust Father God; obeying and acting out His Word (Bible) in daily life, then God will calm your raging storm so that His plan may be completed. Remember everything is done in Father Almighty's timing and way!

Chapter 2 Jealousy and raged can bring out behaviors in people that are strange. You should pray to Father God to ask for wisdom and confidence on what to do. Be confident when speaking the gospel in love. Listen to your Heavenly Father's guidance through His Holy Spirit and act on it immediately. Don't do it on your timing; do it on God's timing because when you trust Father God, He takes care of you. There's a different way out to problems; will you trust and obey Father God in all circumstances? Grow your relationship with God Almighty daily!

Chapter 3 Father God examines your heart and knows when you are passionately serving and obeying Him out of your love for Him. When you have other motives and not reverential fearing God Almighty, Jesus Christ, He knows that you are just performing for others' pleasure. You should strive to know Father God intimately, build your relationship with Him, and acting out His Word (Bible) for all circumstances in life. Don't be afraid to speak up and correct someone when his or her motives are wrong; going against God's Word. Father Almighty's plan will be carried out rightly! Jesus Christ decides where you live forever; in Heaven or the Lake of Fire.

Chapter 4 Sometimes you may want to deepen your relationship with Father God, Jesus Christ, and Holy Spirit. Prayerfully consider what to give up for a set amount of time and grow in love with your first love; Father God, all over again. It won't be easy to do away with this item and Satan will tempt you; making the item desirable, in which you can't resist. Read and study God's Word (Bible) to grow your relationship with God; using it against the enemy but also a guidebook living life honoring Father Almighty. Pray and sing praises to your Lord. Turn on and up worship music in your life. Allow God to get rid of the poisons inside of you and live a joyous life following Father Almighty, Jesus Christ, and Holy Spirit! Get out and help others according to how Jesus helped while living on earth!

Chapter 5 It's time to know God and view yourself as He does; trusting God in all circumstances. Don't lose your faith or hope in your Lord. Seek and desire to know God intimately everyday; He will reveal Himself to you. People don't understand the love, joy, and peace that Father God gives us because we choose to believe in Him. You will be persecuted because of your faith so stand firm in your beliefs when facing opposition. Love and show mercy to everyone, but put your faith into action. Don't add or subtract from the Bible because God has a plan and knows what is beneficial for us. Study Mathew 5 to know how to act that is pleasing to Father God then live it!

Chapter 6 Situations are constantly being thrown at us. Some people enjoy receiving compliments from others way too much. Your aim and desire should be to act how Christ acts and doing what is right according to the Bible. Live for God; giving to others, forgiving, and not worrying about issues because you are trusting Father God. Make a decision not to care what others care about, and care what is pleasing to God. You'll enjoy life and be blessed!

Chapter 7 Lifestyles and interests vary; yet we often have something to be judgmental. God says to speak well of people. Focus on building a relationship with Father God; praying to Him, studying and implementing the Bible in your daily life. Stop acting like everyone else does and begin to help in all circumstances; being intimate with Father God!

Chapter 8 If you have the right heart motives and believe in Jesus Christ, God will perform magnificent miracles in your life. You can trust God so have child-like faith, in which you believed, listened, and performed the action on God's timing; not when you get around to do it. Father God desires you to have an intimate relationship with Him; praying about everything in your life. Focus on Father God; following and trusting Him in every season of life. Bond with God Almighty because it's not enough when you know of Him. He wants you at the wedding feast in Heaven enjoying others' company; not having to be thrown into the Lake of Fire for torment.

Chapter 9 What people don't understand, they criticize or want the item or want the person to leave. But when you are madly in love with Father God and Jesus Christ, you will follow His leading and guidance through His Holy Spirit. Your Father God wants you to live for Him out of your heart, not out of traditions in which you are mindlessly practicing church rituals. Make the most important decision that you'll ever make in your life: believing and living for God your Father, Jesus Christ through His Holy Spirit no matter what. Be determined to follow Father God and to spread His gospel around to people. Share God's love, hope, and His kingdom with others in hopes of them believing and seeing Jesus Christ! Pray to Father God and ask Him how you could increase His kingdom.

Chapter 10 All that people want from this world is to be loved and accepted unconditionally. God has given us, His children, gifts and His characteristics to live in this world. Stand firm and be bold in sharing prophecy (word from Father God,) visions, dreams, laying on the hands for healing people, praying to God in a way that only He can understand, and using Jesus' Name to get rid of demons who are in people. Many people will not accept the message of the gospel because they don't understand who Father God is. Father God wants His children to be diligent and determined in spreading the Bible around to others in gentle and loving ways. You will be persecuted because of your faith in God Almighty, Jesus Christ, and Holy Spirit. Don't give up on speaking of Him because through His Holy Spirit, God will give you the words to say and Jesus is speaking of you to His Father! When your faith, hope, and trust are in Christ Jesus, you know your purpose and how to act in life.

Chapter 11 Help, teach, and preach the Bible to others. Love unconditionally and pray for others. Jesus served everyone all of the time. He loves and speaks the truth. Don't stop loving, praying, or speaking the gospel! Don't expect payment because Father God satisfies all of your needs. If you know Jesus Christ, you know and love Father God!

Chapter 12 Nonsense or no heart emotions attached to worshiping and serving our Lord is not what He desires. When you lend a helping hand or listening ear to others, you should love as Father God loves. Jesus Christ gave His time and attention to everyone. Do good deeds for people because of your love for Father God and continue sharing His gospel! By your words you will be judged by Jesus Christ and what is in your heart; you speak it out. You should choose how to live life and stick with it until the end. Will you act like Father God and Jesus Christ in life or not?

Chapter 13 It's your choice on how much you read and study the Bible, time you spend praying to Father God, and how much you act the Bible out in your daily routines in life. As children of God, we see, hear, and have compassionate hearts so circumstances are viewed differently. Everyone deals with circumstances differently because for some people, they'll believe in, trust, and cling to Father God wholeheartedly. Others will only trust God for a short time, then take over to solve the problem. There are still people who don't believe in Father Almighty and take control in doing whatever they please. Jesus Christ judges everyone. When you die, He decides if you are entering God's kingdom, Heaven or the Lake of Fire forever. Your final destination is coming! Will you be persecuted because of your faith or live life carelessly?

Chapter 14 You have to be confident in your faith in God Almighty, Jesus Christ, and Holy Spirit so you can correct someone whose going against the Bible. Don't be afraid or feel guilty because Father God knows your heart motives and His plan will be completed. You will not understand life's events that happen, but trust and cling to Father God and pray to Him about everything! So don't doubt and continue helping people with God's love!

Chapter 15 Words have an impact in life. They can tear a person down into a deeper sinking hole of depression and rejection. Other words can be uplifting; making people feel loved and hopeful about the future. The words that you speak identify the kind of person you are; reflecting what is in your heart. Don't stop pursuing God Almighty, Jesus Christ, and Holy Spirit with all of your strength. He may not answer you immediately; wanting to see you mature in your faith in Him. So don't give up on seeking and trusting Father God because He will bless you in His timing! Give your all to God Almighty and He will bless you abundantly; just trust Him!

Chapter 16 Father God wants you to rely on Him just as you are because rules and regulations are nonsense. You should follow God's commands found in the New Testament of the Bible. Father God gave His children His power and authority to reign on the earth. If you know of sicknesses, diseases, and demons that are tormenting people or anything that is against the Word of God (Bible,) you can pray to Father God and He will take care of it in His way. You can pray for blessings and God may answer you in His timing. He desires you to want Him to take care of you by being so in love with Him, Father God, Jesus Christ, and Holy Spirit that you don't care what the world says is trendy or what people think of you; your desire is to love God and follow His lead in your life! Life is short so obey His

Holy Spirit's guidance! Jesus determines where you'll live forever; Heaven or the Lake of Fire.

Chapter 17 We have many faith levels so we view situations differently in life. We must be confident in spreading and sharing the gospel with others to the point of death. Jesus gives us a faint picture of what He looks like so hopefully we won't be deceived when He comes back on earth. We have to follow Father God's guidance on how to live life that's pleasing to Him through the guidance of His Holy Spirit. Grow in love and faith with Father God by reading and applying His Word (Bible) in your daily life and praying to Him. He will love, teach, and take care of you! Because of your faith in Jesus Christ, nothing will be impossible for you!

Chapter 18 Children trust, rely on, and cling to their authority figures. When they see them, they rejoice. Children want to be close to their authority figures and are protective, but are fearless at doing new things. They are free to be themselves and they are learning constantly. These behaviors are what Father God desires us to act toward Him. Punishment will come to those who lead people astray from the One true God! When you decide to let Father God to take the control of your life, He and angels rejoice over you! Forgive others because if you don't, Father God doesn't forgive you. How you treat others God will treat you worse because you won't forgive. He knows your heart; if you are being sincere or not. Verse 18 of

Chapter By Chapter

Mathew chapter 18: Father God blesses His children with power and authority through Jesus Christ's Name and Holy Spirit to cast out demons who are torturing people and anything that's against the Bible; you tie it up and throw it into the mist of sea. Also you can pray and can ask for blessings for others. You have to believe and not doubt.

Chapter 19 When your aim, focus, or desire is on worshipping, following, and serving Father God with your whole being, you enjoy and have a blessed life because He satisfies all your needs. You will look to Father God for everything through every season in life. Father God has commandments that are for your well-being and His glorious glory! If you sincerely and deeply love plus are in love with Father God, Jesus Christ, and Holy Spirit, you will bless others by supplying for their needs. Love people by giving. God will reward you in Heaven so practice the Bible in your daily life to be Christ's example to people so they can live for Him!

Chapter 20 Father Almighty equips you with gifts and abilities. You should give the glory to Father God for blessing you with them. Be busy in blessing others and help them to know Father God. Now is the time to act out the true characteristics of God Almighty and Jesus Christ. Be compassionate, merciful, slow to anger, and abounding in love toward others. You need to be willing to have interruptions in your day and help out with the needs of others. Pray to Father God about everything because life doesn't make sense. He will reveal messages, but your ability to comprehend is small so it's important to trust God. He will take care of you. On Judgment Day, Jesus Christ will judge the hearts and lives of people to see if they will enter into Heaven or the Lake of Fire. The last people who die will be first to be judged, which if you are confident in knowing God while you lived on earth, then you know you'll see Him face-to-face and ruling over nations. So you will desire Jesus Christ to judge others because God's children put the needs of others before their own.

Chapter 21 Trust Father God through His guidance of Holy Spirit because everything will be exactly how He planned it. Worshipping Father God, Jesus Christ, and Holy Spirit is a time when you focus on Him; putting everything in your life aside, praying to God, reading the Bible, and listening or singing to worship songs. Too often we can lose sight of the reason for attending church and God desires us to focus on worshipping Him; not treating His church as another social gathering. Express your deepest heart's concern to Father God by praying to Him and in His timing He will answer you in His way; just trust Him and don't doubt. If you want to please Father God, perform the tasks in which He tells you to and when He tells you to. He desires everyone to live in His kingdom so act like Christ so that people will choose to believe in Him and be saved! When you believe in Jesus Christ, He will remove all of

Chapter By Chapter

your brokenness, burdens, addictions, anger, and etc. so He can create you into His own image. This process is a life-long journey and you'll be persecuted because of your faith. But if you don't believe in Jesus Christ, you will experience severe punishment.

Chapter 22 Everyone on earth is invited to the kingdom of God, Heaven, but many will not be entering in. Our King, Jesus Christ knows the reasons why. All those who believe in Him are dressed in His righteousness. As Jesus was tempted and tried, we also will be tempted and tried. The Bible will be twisted so it's important to know Father God and His Word so you can give guidance and correction to others. Be determined to live out your faith in God, Jesus Christ, and Holy Spirit.

Chapter 23 God's children must be willing to teach and yet apply the Bible to others as well as their own lives. It isn't enough to pretend as if you know Father God. People who are like this will teach you things, in which they desire applause and approval from others and yet they don't enjoy completing the grunt work themselves. This is totally and completely not how Father God desires His children to act. He wants you to get your hands dirty so you can love and spread the gospel to others. There aren't rules to enter into Heaven, but believe in your heart and confess with your lips that Jesus Christ is Lord and you shall be saved. God is holy therefore His creation is holy. So you can pretend that you know Father God in front of people, but God knows the real you and what's in your heart. Get rid of judging others and start to develop friendships so that Heaven can increase. God is a God of justice so He will take care of things as He sees fit. You have to be merciful and faithful to Father God as well as others.

Chapter 24 The end of the earth is coming. Verses 6 and 7 of Matthew 24 are already happening frequently. If you are wholeheartedly in love with Father God, Jesus Christ, and Holy Spirit, you'll be persecuted because of your faith in Him. You have to be determined to live out your faith in this wicked world plus continue to love people. Father God gives you warnings and hints on how to distinguish the true end of the age so remember these because it's important! If you know and love Father God, continue acting like Him toward others. You should strive to please Him daily because you never know when Jesus will come back on earth and what better way for Him to see you than seeing you loving others!

Chapter 25 Father God desires you to be anticipating the arrival of your Lord Jesus Christ so when studying the Bible and praying to God; He will help you act like Him toward people. Father God wants you to feed and give water to people, be merciful and compassionate to them, provide clothing, praying for them, and just being their listening ear or shoulder to cry on. Each one of God's children has their own special gifts and abilities that God blessed them with. It's your choice on whether or not you'll bless others by sharing it and giving God the glory. You can decide to just hide your gifts and abilities. Father God will bless your needs abundantly; beyond your comprehension or take away what you do have; leaving you with nothing. So love, pray, and give so that Father God can be proud of you plus say, "well done, good and faithful servant!" Chapter 26 Jesus told His disciples about His death three and four times before the process was started, but they didn't understand. Spending time with people helps you to get to know and love them; yet you know that they'll pass away. Out of your love you will give something to them that each of you will know means tremendously, but to others it will be viewed as a waste. Father God loves you so incredibly much that He gave His Son, Jesus a human body to live on earth for 33 years to be crucified on the cross for you! Jesus Christ knew that people would betray Him, but He never stopped loving or caring for them. Before Judas Iscariot kissed Jesus for Jesus to be arrested, He prayed to Father God. Jesus asked if He could be taken from the crucified situation, yet when He prayed for the second and third time Jesus prayed that Father God's will to be completed. So spend time reading, studying the Bible, praying to God, and acting like Him to people daily. We can't understand everything in life, but we can trust and rely on God to work everything out for His glory!

Chapter 27 Jesus Christ was betrayed, falsely accused, stripped from His clothes, wore a crown of thorns, mocked, spitted at in His face, beaten, flogged, and carried and nailed to the cross. He died a brutal death because of His great and unconditional love for you! He didn't retaliate, but just answered one question. He was treated terribly. Imagine how Father God was feeling through this gruesome process of His only Son who He loves. Jesus felt betrayed, but He died because of His love for you! When you personalize Jesus Christ's death and learn how to act like Him in all of life's circumstances, you decide to be in love with Him, serve and worship Him, and spread His gospel around to others!

Chapter 28 Spread the gospel of your Lord Jesus Christ to people because Father God won't let anything be blocked from knowing Him. There will be oppressors who are trying to block the message of the gospel, but don't be afraid because your Lord your God has gone ahead of you; clearing the path for you. You have to trust Father God, obey Him, and share the joy of your Lord with others! Through His Holy Spirit, God is with you always!

End of <u>Matthew</u>

Chapter By Chapter

Mark

Chapter 1 Don't lose God's joyful excitement and determination to share the good news of Jesus Christ with others! You have to be sincerely sorry for all of your wrongs that you have committed in the past and desire Father God to change you; make you whole. Jesus has been tempted so He knows what you're feeling. You must be willing and in love with Father God and Jesus Christ that you will leave your dearest loved ones behind to follow His leading through His Holy Spirit to share the gospel with others. Go out in Jesus' Name casting out impure spirits, healing the sick, and conversing with God all day long! Give Father God the glory!

Chapter 2 Never stop preaching or teaching the Bible to others. Press through hindrances and oppositions because those opposing forces will always be there. You have to decide if you will be determine to act in faith no matter how hard life gets or to give up. It's time to not let others affect your moods and time to seek Father God with all of your passion! Share the gospel of your Lord and Savior Jesus Christ because everyone needs Him! When you're questioned about your faith, you should be able to give a thorough answer.

Chapter 3 There will be opposition against the Trinity so it's up to you if you'll ignore the accusations and complete God's will; helping others no matter what day it is and casting out evil spirits. Even your closest loved ones will betray Jesus and you so it's important to have an intimate relationship with Father God to rely upon.

Chapter 4 Faith is believing the unseen. Father God wants your heart, soul, and mind trusting Him fully! Life situations don't make sense and you can choose to give God all of control in your life or partial control. You can't keep secrets from Father God so why not grow your relationship with Him to help others know God intimately. Life is brutal, but when you trust in Father God, He calms your storm. Don't lose your faith in Father God because as you continue reading the Bible and praying to Father God daily, He will make Himself known to you. He cares about you, especially, about the teeny-tiny things that concern you!

Chapter 5 God, Jesus, and Holy Spirit is loving. He will take care of you, but you have to want Father God to. If you know that you are God's child, you should be reading your Bible daily and praying to God so that God can glorify Himself through you. Jesus drew people to Himself by acting like Father God so you should be acting like Him in order for people to choose to follow Father God with their whole being. Share your testimony because you may be able to save people some time and money hearing about what God has done for you. So what if it doesn't fit in your schedule. God and Jesus is important so obey His Holy Spirit's lead. You will resume to your set task eventually. Give God the glory when He has answered your prayers or performed miracles!

Chapter 6 Depending on your family's background, you may be the only child of God in your family who has an intimate relationship with Father God, Jesus Christ, and Holy Spirit. Share the message of your Lord Jesus Christ and you'll be persecuted or mocked because of your faith so continue to share and act out your faith every moment in life. If people accept the message of the gospel, God's peace will rest on them. But if they deny Christ, God's peace won't rest on them for a blessed life. Life is a crazy-roller-coaster-ride and you don't know which way you are turning. If you let God lead you through His Holy Spirit, you will enjoy serving Him and people because you know that God is faithful to provide for your needs.

Chapter 7 In society, there is pressure to be in the "in crowd" that people will say and do anything just to "fit in." Stop it because God desires true passionate worship and following His plan for your life in the core of your heart; not phony jibber-jabber or going through the motions of looking like God's child when really you're not. Words and actions portray what's in your heart so sexual immorality, theft, murder, adultery, and evil thoughts are depictions of you if you have conversations regarding these topics. It's time to act out your beliefs and share them with others. Don't be afraid; just let God glorify Himself through you!

Chapter 8 God's children are undeserving in receiving God Almighty's unfailing love and blessings. We need to believe in and trust God because He will take care of us. By His power and authority, God does miracles. We just have to ask in prayer, continue seeking God, and acting how He wants us to act from a pure fiery-heart zealous passion. Don't do religious rules because God desires a relationship with the uniquely you, not strict rules that turn you into a mindless robot. God wants you to share your whole heart and life with Him in daily prayer about everything! Decide that you're unashamed of God, Jesus, and Holy Spirit so that you can follow Him daily because the cares of this world are worthless. Let God do miracles through you when you boldly speak of Him to others!

Chapter 9 All of creation will see Jesus Christ when He comes to earth in our Father's glory. But God's children must be in constant communication with Father God so He can do His will within us. Talk to God because He knows how much faith you have in Him and will know how much of Himself to reveal to you. It's a slow process of building your relationship with God, but it's worth it to be in love with Him daily. Love, help, and share the gospel with others, but remember to keep a healthy relationship with God so you are prepared in sharing the gospel effectively!

Chapter 10 Jesus created everyone to display God's characteristics so that all of creation would have an intimate relationship with Father God. Father God loves you unconditionally, but desires you to want Him to lavish His almighty love on you. God wants you to want to love Him daily; building a strong relationship in which you fully depend on Him that your love for Him can't be broken. You have to be willing to give up total control in your life so that God can complete His plan for your life. You just have to trust and obey Him because giving up your desires and following God is the best. All things are possible with God! You don't know and have a small understanding of what life entails so that's why it's important to rely on God, Jesus, and Holy Spirit. Pray to God about everything because you'll face trials and persecution because of your faith in God. He will bless you abundantly if your heart is rightly devoted to Him!

Chapter 11 Father God wants you to obey and trust Him through every season in life. When you do obey and trust Father God; pushing aside your fears and self-centered desires, you'll experience God's awesome plan. You will have joy, love, and peace making you want to worship and follow Father God with a fiery-passion in your heart. Be careful not to be a fake child of the Most High God, in which your appearance seems to be correct, but your heart isn't intimate with Father God at all. God knows your heart and will take care of you as He sees fit.

Pray to God whatever is on your heart and believe that He hears you. Forgiveness can be hard to do, but when you remember all of what Jesus has done for you, it makes you decide to forgive loved ones because you're madly in love with Father God! Share God and His Word with everyone!

Chapter 12 It's your choice on whether or not you will apply God's Word and the lessons that Father God has taught you in your daily life. You'll have to decide to give up all of your anger, brokenness, hurt, and addictions to let Father God heal you from the inside out. It's time to stop running away from God and start running toward Him with all of your soul, mind, understanding, and strength to become in love with God! Seek God wholeheartedly and act how you know how Father God wants you to; pay attention to what God says and less attention to others' views. There's only one true God. Love and give to others out of your true love passion for Father God, Jesus Christ, and Holy Spirit! Don't let anything stop you.

Chapter 13 Being fully confident in the Lord can be difficult. The Holy Spirit will speak through you if you're devoted to Christ. Jesus is coming back, but this world will continue to get worse. Deceivers will deceive many so it's important to know the Word of God! He reveals signs about what's still coming. Listen with God's ears and see!

Chapter 14 Actions become memories. People can choose to live for Christ (being led by the Spirit) or be pushed around by others. The memories have positive and negative outcomes are different for everybody. The Holy Spirit will remind God's children of things, but we have a choice to obey or not to. He'll remind you just so long until He stops because of your disobedience. Keep God's eyes, ears, and compassionate heart always in your daily life!

Chapter 15 The process of Jesus being crucified was horrendous! People plotted against Him, beat, flogged, betrayed, falsely accused, mocked, striped His clothes, and spit in His face. Jesus answered a few questions, but for the rest of the time He remained silent! We should have a close and intimate relationship with God our Father; praying and remaining silent while being persecuted. He forgives us of all our sins so we can and should forgive others!

Chapter 16 Where is your faith level or how much faith do you have in our Lord Jesus Christ? Do you believe in God our Father, Christ the Son, and the Holy Spirit? Proclaim and live out your faith through actions. In the Name of Jesus, you can preach the gospel of Christ, drive out demons, speak in tongues, and lay hands on people to have them get well. Holy Spirit does miracles by God's will!

End of <u>Mark</u>

Chapter By Chapter

Luke

Chapter 1 God Almighty hears the prayers of the righteous! When you pray and live life-glorifying Christ, He hears and knows the desires of your heart. You can doubt or choose to believe things unseen. You can praise and worship God by singing in the early stages when things appear to be the same or at the end when the blessing is visible. Endure trials with God and remember He's molding you for His purpose plus spiritual growth!

Chapter 2 The Holy Spirit tells God's children snippets. His snippets can be ahead of time, in which leaves God's children knowing what the next step will be and when it'll happen. Often people will try to remember certain aspects, but end up forgetting it. Learning, asking questions, and studying God's Word are important! Yearn after God, Jesus, and the Holy Spirit for spiritual growth!

Chapter 3 Trials come and we need to endure them with the Holy Spirit because He's strengthening us for our journey. In the desert can be a time of learning if you seek God wholeheartedly. Put into practice and make God's Word your lifestyle! Give without expecting anything in return, quit setting high standards for others, and live passionately for Christ! Glorify Him in everything!

Chapter 4 Satan is the evil temper and may use God's Word (Bible) against you. As Jesus shows, we need to know and use the Word as a sword properly. Hometowns are great, but a person isn't honored or respected as if he or she were in another town. Act out God's Word, follow the Holy Spirit's guidance, and be ready at all times!

Chapter 5 Routine tasks are completed, but some do not turn out. The Holy Spirit dwells inside of God's children. God wants His children to obey, trust, and follow Him. You have a choice to follow the Holy Spirit's guidance without arguing or to continue thinking you have control. When you're worn out, just pray because God sees and knows everything. He'll answer prayers in His timing and way! Be available to Christ and the Holy Spirit always! He can do miracles!

Chapter 6 People are known by their actions. Stop trying to impress others because that becomes exhausting. By your words is the reflection of what's in your heart. Speak positively, you have a positive outlook or speak negatively; you have a negative outlook. The power of life and death is in the tongue! You'll be judged but how you lived is important. Are you living for yourself trying to climb the success ladder by cheating or hurting others? Do you live for Christ; lending, helping, crying with others, and aren't ashamed living for Christ? Love as God loves you, pray for your enemies, give without expecting, be merciful, don't judge, and share your testimony! Study God's Word and build a firm foundation with

God our Father, Christ the Son, and the Holy Spirit! Put God's Word into practice in your life.

Chapter 7 In society, often people expect repayment or reactions from others. It's time to give and help without expecting. Give without limitations because it's a joy! People may speak well of you on your behalf. Remember, God may use you to bring others in His kingdom. Grow in love with our Father Almighty and act His love out in your life!

Chapter 8 God is in control. Trials spin into motion and then disappear. We have choices to make. We can worry, loose God's peace and joy or trust God. We won't understand or enjoy circumstances in our lives, but believing in Father Almighty, Jesus Christ is what matters! Share how God changed you! Let His light shine and glorify God in your life. Life isn't easy or a cakewalk so journey with the Holy Spirit leading you!

Chapter 9 God provides for your needs so trust, obey, and follow His commands. People won't accept your beliefs so don't shy away because they are mocking God our Father and Jesus Christ. God will bless you if you wholeheartedly seek Him by studying His Word and obey His Holy Spirit to live Christ-like. Don't look back or conform to the worldly actions. Seek and aim for God's kingdom!

Chapter 10 Spread and act out the Word of God. God created you for His purpose, but you need to surrender control and submit to Him. Be available to the Holy Spirit's lead and guidance because God may use you to draw people into a relationship with Himself. Love our Father Almighty, love others, and be compassionate in all things! Study God's Word to learn how to live for Christ! Nothing can separate you from the love of God!

Chapter 11 Prayer and endurance are important. Sometimes we have to show Father Almighty that we mean business. Act justly, love mercy, and do God's will. Religion has rules that are hindrances. Seek God, Jesus Christ, and the Holy Spirit because He'll guide you to the Truth! Ways to know that we are children of God are by actions, in eyes, and words we speak. Stop giving orders and just love like Christ loves!

Chapter 12 Be on your guard and know God's Word because Satan wants to throw you off from the straight and narrow path, which leads to eternal life (Heaven). Fear, love, and respect God Almighty! This world won't satisfy you so glorify God in your life by seeking/praying to Him and helping others, and giving your supplies over to bless them. You must do it with a sincere heart! God provides for your needs. Treasure God, Jesus Christ, and the Holy Spirit in your heart! God will give blessings if you continue to do His will no matter the cost until the End! Jesus judges you fairly!

Chapter 13 With the deepest sincerity in your heart, repent of your sins and believe in our Lord Jesus Christ. The Holy Spirit will help you know what's pleasing to God and you have a choice whether to obey or not. Live life that glorifies God in everything! If you choose Christ, He'll make you new (getting rid of anger, jealousy, pride, hard-heart, lying, cheating, and etc.) from the inside out. Once your baggage from the inside is gone, you'll be continuing traveling down on the narrow path. You need to seek God, study His Word, and act Christ-like in your life to fragrance Him in this dark world. The Holy Spirit will help if you listen. God fights for you. If you choose not to live for God, He won't know you and you'll be sent to Hell and the Lake of Fire.

Chapter 14 As children of God, we're going to be tested and judged harshly than people who aren't living for Christ. When someone invites you to dinner, pick the less honorable seat to avoid embarrassment. If the host wants you to move to an honorable spot, the host will move you up. This same circumstance happens in God's hands so be humble and He will exalt you in a higher position. Become friends with all sorts of people but don't compromise your faith. You will realize how much God has blessed you with! Continue to be Christ's light and salt in your deeds and words! Sometimes relationships need a change so that your devotion to God, Jesus, and Holy Spirit is pure and strong!

Chapter 15 When you choose Jesus Christ as your personal Lord and Savior, there's rejoicing in Heaven. Repent because God is waiting with arms wide open. God is a gentleman so He won't force Himself on you. When you realize that you don't have any control over your life and have reached your rock bottom, go to Father Almighty because His love and compassion are what you need. You need God and everything that He has is yours! Walk in love, joy, peace, patience, goodness, kindness, and self-control as your relationship with God grows intimate.

Chapter 16 It's easy to treat someone; relation of that person, or friends with that person awful because he or she stabbed you in the back. God doesn't want you to play this game because unbelievers play this. Pray and bless your enemies. Your relationship with God is important than playing revenge as the world does. Our Father blesses His children so don't screw that up because God will take it away. Be devoted to God, Jesus, and the Holy Spirit because He satisfies you. Money will perish and the End is coming. Be Christ's example in this dark world. Heaven or the Lake of Fire is waiting. The choice is yours!

Chapter 17 Sometimes you expect compliments or different outcomes to happen, but in reality you shouldn't expect. If you run after money, jealousy, using people, and drugs, your life will be in turmoil. You'll have nobody to blame, but yourself! You have a choice whether or not act Christ-like in your life and allow the Holy Spirit to mature you. Listen and obey Him because Jesus and God's kingdom are coming back. Seek our

Father Almighty and continue to study God's Word to know how to act.

Chapter 18 Prayer is powerful and we must respect our Lord. He answers our prayers in His timing and way so some prayers will be unanswered. The Holy Spirit will defend, protect, and avenge according to God's will for you. Don't boast about yourself to our Father. Be humble and confident while praying because you'll have peace and God will exalt you in something. Your intimate relationship with Father Almighty and Jesus Christ should be important that you'd leave everything behind to build your faith! God reveals messages to His children sometimes ahead of time, but in ignorance we don't understand. Pray continuously and you need to be waiting on God patiently!

Chapter 19 As children of God, we must be eager and passionate in helping others. Seek guidance from the Holy Spirit and He'll tell you what to do or what not to do based upon your obedience. Don't let a bump in the road discourage you from quitting, but pray to God because He's on your side. Trials should be focusing on embracing God and strengthening your faith in Him. Put your beliefs in your lifestyle. When Jesus told His disciples about His death, His death happened 9 days after that conversation. So take a long look in your life to ponder and pray for clarity. Praise God always!

Chapter 20 You'll be questioned based upon your faith. For some people it's easy to trust others, but others have difficulties trusting people. That's why it's important to put your trust in God. He makes all things new, but it's a slow process. He's the Master, but is gentle and has unending love for you! He will transform you from healing your brokenness to knowing you are God's treasure! Pray honestly and study His Word (Bible). He desires an intimate relationship with you and He will place the right people on your path to strengthen your faith. Be determined, but you have to trust and obey God! Be sensitive in building a relationship with God and not a religion.

Chapter 21 When you're hurting, God, Jesus, and the Holy Spirit is whom you need to rely on. When finances are to the bare bones, relationships are in shambles, and nothing seems to be working properly, that's when your faith in God should grow stronger. Make a choice to put your faith and trust in God Almighty no matter what. Everything will be wiped away from earth. There won't be anyone to help, not even loved ones because there will be division in relationships. Share your God-written testimony along with God's wisdom through His Holy Spirit, but don't worry, He speaks through you if you're living for Christ with all of your being! God tells His children signs that will and are happening in the End Times. Study His Word (Bible) and build a relationship with Father God, Jesus Christ, and the Holy Spirit. Pray that you won't be deceived when Jesus comes back on the earth. Stand firm for Jesus!

Chapter 22 Jesus created the earth. He spent time with people even though He knew that betrayal was coming. Yet He still loved, showed mercy, and had compassion. As His children, we should be acting this same way; loving and having mercy toward others. God knows everything even when Satan knocks us off of the narrow path that leads to the kingdom of God (Heaven). Our bodies are weak and don't obey in serving or loving others, but act self-centered. The Holy Spirit will help you on your journey. Listen and obey because life in Jesus Christ is exciting, thrilling, and lasts forever!

Chapter 23 All that you have to do to be saved is believe that Jesus Christ is Lord with all of your heart and confess Him with your lips! You'll enter into Heaven when your citizenship expires on earth. Jesus Christ's death was for you to save you. You're a sinner, but God, Jesus, and the Holy Spirit complete you. You're perfect in God's eyes and one-day-soon you will see what God sees in you! Ask for the Holy Spirit to dwell within you for wisdom and understanding to live life-glorifying God!

Chapter 24 Ask God to bless you with boldness and confidence to speak about God our Father, Christ the Son, and the Holy Spirit with people. Your intimate relationship with God should be bubbling outside of you because you are compassionate about your Lord Jesus Christ! Have the excitement in your soul for Him that comes out in a lifestyle? You can't contain a fire once it's blazing so this is what the Holy Spirit should be doing in you. Speak and act, but in obedience and humility, Christ-like with the Holy Spirit's guidance! The Holy Spirit gives you power and authority from God in the Name of Jesus.

End of <u>Luke</u>

John

Chapter 1 When you are in a dark room, once you turn the light on, the darkness vanishes. When your electronics aren't working, you need to plug them into the power circuit to have them working again. Many people don't understand that they need Jesus. In darkness, you stumble and fall because you can't see and you don't have control. You don't have recognition of anything. This is the same thing when Jesus created the earth. People didn't and continue not to recognize that they need an intimate relationship with God our Father, Christ the Son, and the Holy Spirit. Speak of God our Father, Christ the Son, and the Holy Spirit everyday. Pray to God and study His Word (Bible) daily. He builds your faith when your faith, hope, trust, and love are established or rooted in Him! Believe in God our Father, Christ the Son, and the Holy Spirit!

Chapter 2 When you rely on or in something, you trust in and cling to it. Jesus desires to have you trust in, cling to, and rely on Him with your whole heart! Be honest and pray to God Almighty because He knows where your faith level is at with Him. He desires compassionate heart-thrives children who follow God our Father, Christ the Son, and the Holy Spirit! He wants you to seek Him with your entire being so get away from religion and people pleasing. Everything should be in agreement and have corrections completed according to what God's Word says! Believe, begin, and grow your intimate relationship with God our Father, Christ the Son, and the Holy Spirit!

Chapter 3 Many people enjoy darkness because it covers up aspects that they don't want to be seen. When you believe and confess that Jesus Christ is Lord, you're getting rid of burdens and coming in His light plus eternal life! Once you do, you will enjoy building an intimate relationship with Him and the Holy Spirit will counsel you on the ways of acting Christ-like. You will give up the control in life and follow His lead in life because you will be deeply in love with Jesus! If you don't believe in Him, you will experience God's wrath and end up in Hell and the Lake of Fire.

Chapter 4 Often you can't pinpoint what you are craving for so you begin the trial and error method. You need to come to the point of the end of yourself and surrender to God; in allowing Him to satisfy you. As children of God, we need to be acting out in love, joy, peace, patience, goodness, kindness, and self-control. Sometimes we need to be blunt in love with others in hopes of them seeing the truth. We are Christ's examples so take action with the Holy Spirit's guidance and share your God-written testimony with others expanding the kingdom of God!

Chapter 5 You have to walk-the-walk and talk-the-talk with determination. You can't be a pushover or else, someone will walk pass you. Make a decision to believe in the Lord Jesus Christ, seek guidance from the Holy Spirit to do God's will, and spread the gospel. Jesus will judge on Judgment Day that which is pleasing to Father God. He has a plan and will bring it to completion so be His light in this dark world until the End of Time!

Chapter 6 Sometimes Jesus tests you in how you will react in circumstances, but remember He has a plan and knows what He will do. Many people attract to items and others because they show signs that are pleasing. God our Father and Jesus don't want this; people believing in a cause of many signs. God and Jesus want people believe out of a willing/sincere heart that Jesus Christ is Lord! God wants everyone to be saved and have eternal life. Your soul is longing for Jesus because He satisfies. If you are striving for self-ambition, it won't satisfy and counts for nothing. If you believe in and confess Jesus Christ is Lord, you'll be saved.

Chapter 7 Take a step back and decide if whom you are, is for your own glory or to glorify God. Will you stand in truth to glorify God or will you say it's all about you? People can pressure you down a winding road of success, but they may not believe in your gift. They may change you so you have to decide what you want and who you are. If you believe in Jesus Christ, the Holy Spirit dwells within you if you ask Him to. Jesus is living water that satisfies your soul and gives the Holy Spirit to help you to live life that is pleasing to God!

Chapter 8 It's easy to be judgmental and to think nothing is wrong with us. If you believe in Jesus, He takes away your sins and remembers them no more. Your focus should be on Christ and by the Holy Spirit; He helps you understand whom God is and how to act if you are obedient to the Holy Spirit. Again, will you stand in truth to glorify God or will you say it's all about you? Stop being two-faced because you're a liar when you are! If you believe in Jesus, you know God and so obey His Word! Be proud that you are God's child and act like Him in life!

Chapter 9 We don't understand the reasons behind life's circumstances unfolding. We can step out in faith that God will do what He wants. Time is becoming shorter until the day that Jesus comes back again on the earth. As children of God, we need to be spreading the gospel. No one else can spread or act like Christ as you can. Others may not stand up for Jesus. God created you unique! You have a purpose that God made for you and only you can fulfill it. So believe, study, obey, and follow the Holy Spirit to do God's will. If you believe in Jesus but don't love or help, you are guilty of knowing Christ. Act how you want to be judged by Jesus!

Chapter 10 There is no sneaking in or a back door to eternal life, Heaven. The only way to have eternal life, go to Heaven is by believing in Jesus. As children of God, we know His voice because He calls each one of us by our name. He leads us by His Holy Spirit, but remember, Jesus has gone before us in life. You are in Jesus Christ's hands! Take action in seeking God, Jesus, and obeying the Holy Spirit because you are His example to the world. The way you live glorifying, honoring, and praising God may expand the kingdom of God! So live justly, love mercy, and walk humbly before God!

Chapter 11 Life is full of instances where everything is falling apart. You may have to mend relationships that otherwise you would rather not. You may be in a horrendous trial of your life: a loved one barely surviving. In the midst of your pain and heartache, God is working to glorify His Son Jesus Christ plus strengthening your faith, love, and trust in Him! Everything works in His perfect timing! Pour your heart out to God because He hears your prayers if you believe in Jesus!

Chapter 12 Expansive cars, money, clothes, jewelry, relationships, and houses are some of the luxuries that people think will satisfy them. Many people, if they're honest, aren't satisfied when they have these luxuries. When people believe in and serve the Lord Jesus Christ, they will have eternal life! As children of God, we know or at least should know who God is because Jesus is His example. Be ready to be judged on the last day!

Chapter 13 You can make a choice to love. When you know and love God, Jesus, and obey the Holy Spirit, you are His example to the world. The moments that you don't want to be kind continue to love because you are making an impact in God's kingdom. Many of you want to be in charge, but I challenge you not to have authority that's abusive. Why not include others in the decision-making and stop belittling them? Show others that you don't think highly of yourself by completing unfavorable tasks. God's love is indescribable and so act out His love in all circumstances, but remember many people will not like you because of your faith in Jesus Christ!

Chapter 14 No one has seen Father Almighty, but Jesus is preparing Heaven for all those who believe in Him. If you believe in Jesus, you believe in and know Father God. Jesus does His Father's will. The Holy Spirit is a gift from God whom teaches and reminds you how to live life glorifying Father Almighty. Show how much you love God and Jesus by obeying His commands. In return, He will lavish His love on you!

Chapter 15 By keeping God's commands and serving Him out of the love that's in your heart, He will pour out His love on you! Each passing day and year, hopefully your relationship with God strengthens! Father God prunes you if you believe in Jesus so that He can be glorified in your life. Pruning isn't always easy because some branches can be difficult than others. Throwing away greed and selfishness can be branches that God wants to prune because they are not His characteristics. Life without God is meaningless and you won't have His unfailing love, hope, joy or peace that goes beyond understanding! If you believe in Jesus, He calls you friend because He reveals our Father's business, characteristics, and desires on how to live glorifying Him! You will be persecuted because of your faith so don't be alarmed and continue to testify in love!

Chapter 16 You will be persecuted because of your faith in Jesus Christ. If you believe in Jesus and received the Holy Spirit, He teaches and reminds of the ways of God. In this world, you will have trouble Jesus says, but don't worry He has overcome the world. So troubles won't harm you because Jesus has conquered them for you. His death conquered them and God fights for you. So believe in, trust in Jesus Christ, and obey the Holy Spirit!

Chapter 17 When you believe in Jesus Christ, His death makes you holy. You are set apart from living a mess-up life, such as alcohol, drugs, partying, having sex outside of marriage etc. Communicate in prayer to your Father in your simple unique communication style. God has all power and authority! He has given His children the gift of His Holy Spirit to help us live in the world. Trials come, but you can either choose to seek God so He can mature your faith or be stressed. He blesses you with unspeakable joy and peace when you praise Father God!

Chapter 18 Jesus Christ didn't hide when He was being arrested before He was crucified. He knew who would deny knowing Him three times and who would betray Him for the means of handing Him over to die. Yet Jesus Christ was compassionate to people who were apart of the process of crucifying Him. We should confront problems in a gentle and determined way. Voice your opinion appropriately in love!

Chapter 19 Power comes from God. Some people don't want to see you suffer, but if you believe in Jesus, He is whom you cling to. People can be a snob and you just don't want to deal with that kind of behavior. Try to be compassionate during trials. Empty your heart to God in prayer. Looking back on trials, you may understand and see the glory of God in the trial.

Chapter 20 Sometimes God our Father will choose you as His means of comforting people. God may reveal Himself to them through you as you are being compassionate that's sincere. It may be years before they realize it was God, the Holy Spirit and believe in Him! Run and pray to God because He comforts you like nobody else can! You have to believe with your heart and confess with your lips that Jesus Christ is your Lord and Savior and you shall be saved! You will find life is worth living for when you honor and praise God in it!

Chapter 21 You can be taught wrongly about God and His Word (Bible). To make sure that you are traveling down on the right path, get a Bible, open and read it, ask questions, pray, study, and re-read the Bible. Walk out into deep waters to ask difficult questions because with sincerity in your heart, God will answer you in His way! Building your intimate faith relationship, God may use you to be His spokesperson to grow

His Heavenly kingdom. Do you love God with fiery excited passion in your heart that you'll be willing to be persecuted to death, out of your faith in Jesus Christ? You need to with confidence, boldly speak of God our Father, Christ the Son, and the Holy Spirit in your unique communication style! Don't try to be someone else. Just be yourself and don't let others manipulate you!

End of John

Acts

Chapter 1 The Holy Spirit will teach you and remind you of how to act like Jesus and His teachings. If you believe in Jesus Christ, you are His example on how to love, forgive, give, and showing mercy in this world. Share your testimony on how God has transformed your life. God chooses the unfavorable person to glorify Himself. Pray and testify about God, Jesus, and Holy Spirit!

Chapter 2 The Holy Spirit enables you to speak and pray in different languages. This speaking in different languages is called speaking in tongues and is for encouragement or warnings for the future and is a word from God. You should study the Bible, pray, and ask questions to be a passionate spokesperson for the Lord. In doing so, you may have chances to correct people in their misunderstandings of faith. They may disagree, but all that you can do is speak and act out the Truth (gospel) in love in hopes of expanding God's kingdom!

Chapter 3 These opinions will be from having Cerebral Palsy and being nonverbal. I have become used to having people stare at me. Often when I drool uncontrollably or when I'm eating in public, many people are grossed out or appalled by my messy routines. Instances in which they are uncomfortable speaking to me, they will either ignore me or speak to me as if I'm a toddler. I become immune in having conversations because I become tired of the stereotypical behaviors. I always have the "small talk" conversations with people, but that's it. Often there is a lack in eye contact between parties as shown in Acts 3 that I become used to not looking at people in the eye because of the stereotypical behaviors that it becomes a norm. Be someone who breaks out of the status quote and strike up a conversation with the special needs in making eye contact. Act in God's merciful and compassionate love. If you have faith in Jesus Christ and believe in Him, His Name is powerful! If it's God's will, He will answer your prayers to be healed, but don't doubt! Praise, worship, and testify about Jesus in your daily life!

Chapter 4 You don't have to be highly-educated to be God's servant or even have the pictured-perfect life. People have many viewpoints on what a pictured-perfect life looks like so take a moment and imagine this life. God's children need to and should be bold in speaking about Jesus Christ to people. You may think that you have nothing going for you to testify about God Almighty and Jesus Christ to expand His kingdom. But God may use you to glorify Himself through your life. You will be persecuted so be bold in testifying about God, Jesus, and Holy Spirit! Don't quit when it's difficult. Pray to God. He will give you the gift of the Holy Spirit if your heart is rightly devoted to Christ and obeys God! When this happens, God will speak through you in His wisdom and knowledge.

Chapter 5 The Holy Spirit will give you God Almighty's wisdom, understanding, and discernment. Will you speak up to confront people when the Holy Spirit alerts you? Many of you need to expand your faith boundaries and quit looking for people's approvals on your life. It's time to love God intimately and compassionately so that when you are persecuted for Jesus Christ, you find joy! You shouldn't be discouraged, but God fights for you so the battle has already been won! You'll see the victory, but you have to be devoted to Jesus! Never stop spreading the Word of God around in the world!

Chapter 6 If ministry time is lacking in your life or you see people not having their needs met properly, it's time for a change. Maybe you need to quit something to spread the Word of God around rapidly. You need to pray to God and listen to His Holy Spirit's guidance. Someone else or a group of people may be chosen for the ministry so you need to have a positive attitude about he or she. Don't be jealous! Of course, opposition and persecution will happen when ministering for Jesus Christ. There's a time to speak and a time to be silent so that God is glorified.

Chapter 7 The topic of the Holy Spirit seems to be touchy because many people have the lack of knowledge about Him. The Holy Spirit is in you (if you ask Father God for this gift) by leading, guiding, teaching, and reminding you the ways of God. If God wants you to have wisdom and understanding in certain circumstances, His Holy Spirit will give you the words to say. Be bold and don't be afraid because the Holy Spirit is within you! Let your heart be devoted to Christ! Life doesn't make sense, but with God, all things are possible!

Chapter 8 Sometimes God may choose to use people to strengthen your faith in Him. The Holy Spirit is a gift from God that money can't buy. Ask in prayer for the Holy Spirit because God gives you wisdom and understanding, but you have to listen to that still small voice. Repent in prayer with a sincere heart of all your sins and God remembers them no longer. God may use you to speak His gospel to people so obey the guidance of His Holy Spirit to win souls to expand the kingdom of God (Heaven). Speak to them on their faith level.

Chapter 9 Someone can be against having faith in Jesus Christ. He or she can speak negatively about God and think that people who believe in Jesus Christ are phonies, hypocrites, and using an excuse in dealing with life problems by oneself. When God our Father, Jesus Christ, and Holy Spirit intervenes, He changes someone's heart and life around to display His glory! Don't judge because God uses His people to bring glory to Him and to increase His kingdom. Pray constantly and God will display His glory so don't be afraid during trials! Trust and obey His Holy Spirit.

Chapter 10 The Holy Spirit tells Father God what God's children are doing on the earth. God hears your prayers so why not love and respect Him with your whole being? God may give you a word, which is called prophecy or a dream or a vision. Many of you think that when prophecy, dream or vision happen the result or message happens immediately. God works in His timing, not yours. So it may take days, weeks, months, or years before you see the result happen. Grow in love with God, help others, and testify about Jesus Christ! All people can be saved, just by believing in Jesus Christ. There isn't favoritism. The choice is yours whether or not to believe in Jesus Christ!

Chapter 11 People who are African-American, Muslim, Baptist, Reformed, Christian Reformed, Catholic, Greek, Jew, Lutheran, and etc. can be saved by believing in Jesus Christ. As believers, we often slip into and have a mindset of attaining blank title is the only "right" way to get to Heaven and live on earth. We become bigheaded in pointless conversations instead of focusing on God Almighty, Jesus Christ, and Holy Spirit. Strip away the judgmental and egoistic mind frames to share God's Word not adding or subtracting to it. You can't stand in God's way to avoid people from believing in Jesus Christ, but you can be a hindrance. Persecution will come and you should take a stand for God to speak of Him when you wholeheartedly believe in Jesus.

Chapter 12 During life's trials, it's easy to lose track of God because our focus isn't on Him. Most often our focus is surrounded in our trial, which causes worry, stress, and etc. Praying to God and expressing your heart's cry to Him is what He desires! God can change your circumstance, but you have to trust and obey Him. He will do unbelievable things that only He can do. When you are trapped and everything is against you, pray to God and praise Him! Share your testimony about God with others so that His kingdom (Heaven) can increase!

Chapter 13 People will mock you and Jesus Christ because they don't know Him. Insults will be spoken and there are people as well as evil spirits working against God to keep others away from reaching Heaven. Will you be the person who doesn't stop sharing that salvation is in our Lord Jesus Christ during persecution and opposition? Speak up and share God's wisdom and truth! If the message of Jesus Christ isn't welcomed or accepted, God's peace will not rest on those people so shake the dust off of your feet. This is to say that they are choosing to ignore God. God's peace will be with you instead of blessing others with His peace. Don't be discouraged when they don't believe. All you can do is pray to God, read and study the Bible, love, and share the gospel with all people!

Chapter 14 Anger and holding someone on a high-platform are dangerous. Being angry can cause problems, but God will give you the ability and strength to confront problems. You should explain to others that you aren't on a high-platform and that you are passionately in love with God and Jesus Christ. Speak of

God and Jesus passionately with others! Stand firm in the faith to avoid having regret when seeing Jesus face-to-face.

Chapter 15 Misunderstanding of the Bible and God, Jesus, and Holy Spirit leads to misinterpreting. Speak when you know a faith topic profoundly. You may be the one who God chooses to use to explain the gospel, His love, and salvation to people. Are you ready to share at the spur of the moment? Lend a helping hand to others while being an encouragement!

Chapter 16 Sometimes God may allow you to go to a place to lead people to Christ for salvation, but also, there are times that God doesn't want you to go to spread the gospel. God may give you a vision to answer you about something. You will be persecuted for your faith in Jesus Christ. Persecution for Christ isn't fair, but it's well worth it, seeing God and Jesus face-to-face when the time comes! Will you continue to pray and praise God in the mist of the chaos? In the mist of the chaos, people may choose Jesus Christ as their Lord and Savior! I hope you are ready to pray with them at that moment.

Chapter 17 Educate yourself on the Word of God by reading and studying it everyday. Ponder it and God will reveal Himself to you and how He wants you to live on earth. Explain the Word of God to others. Creation and people are God's testimony that He's real and His love is great! There are many distractions that hold people from having a relationship with

God, Jesus, and Holy Spirit. Make a choice to develop a relationship with God, Jesus, and Holy Spirit now!

Chapter 18 Will you be courageous to keep on speaking about God our Father, Jesus Christ, and Holy Spirit in the trials as well as in the joyous moments? Don't become weary about speaking of Him with others. God may choose to speak through someone else, but always, be ready to testify about Christ. You are safe in God's hands and God will place people in your life to strengthen your faith. Learn and speak out the Word of God. Know the Word of God so that you can explain issues thoroughly to others!

Chapter 19 The Holy Spirit enables you to have power and authority to speak in tongues and to prophesy. These are two gifts out of the nine gifts from what God will give you when you ask for His Holy Spirit. Don't think too highly of yourself because God gives you the ability to heal the sick by the laying on of hands, cast out evil spirits who are in people in the Name of Jesus, speak in tongues, and to prophesy. Repent of wrongs you have committed by praying and asking forgiveness from God. Know and be able to explain your beliefs. Sometimes silence is all that's needed to glorify God.

Chapter 20 Encourage one another to motivate them to do great things for God. Even though hardships, persecutions, and oppositions come, your love for God should be so intimate that you can speak of Him all of the day long! Don't be afraid to pray with others. Aim to know God by reading and studying the Word of God (Bible) to avoid being deceived and leading people astray. Love and bless others!

Chapter 21 When you have an intimate relationship with God and Jesus Christ, you will go to great lengths, even to death, to speak of and share about God our Father and Jesus! People may pray for you and prophesy over you. Warnings to stop sharing and preaching the gospel may come, but you have a choice whether or not to continue on being a spokesperson for your Lord. Encouragement and strengthening to share the gospel comes by studying God's Word, praying to God, and having relationships with believers!

Chapter 22 Conversational topics are infinite, but some children of God don't share how God transformed their lives. We all have a past so share your testimony rather than a mundane conversational topic. If we choose to believe and confess that Jesus Christ is Lord, we should be studying His Word and praying to God. Spend quality time with God! The Holy Spirit will help you to speak God's Word. You never know how God will produce His seed in others, but His children must be willing to scattered His seed. Stop being afraid and just love people with God's love. God will take care of you!

Chapter 23 Doubts and nerves can knock you off of the Lord's plan for your life. The second guessing game starts in your mind. It's important to thoroughly know God, know who you are, know God loves you, and know God's character to act it out in life. God knows everything about you! You need to take a breather to know that God is comforting you through His Spirit in a way that's special to you. He will calm the storm and trial that you are in, but you have to trust God. In God's way, everything works out!

Chapter 24 When people are mocking and falsely accusing you because they know that you're God's child, you can be mad or continue sharing Christ's resurrection with them. You will be tested because of your faith in God our Father, Jesus Christ, and Holy Spirit. Many people understand and remember things better when aspects are relatable to their lives so try to incorporate this technique when spreading the Word of God to them. Your love and faith in God should be intimate that you won't accept payment or bribes. Remember you are God's representation of Himself in this fallen world and you may help God in expanding Heaven. This may take years for people to choose Jesus Christ so continue to love, pray, and share the gospel in all aspects of life.

Chapter 25 Have a clean conscious. God makes ways for you to avoid terrible danger. This doesn't mean that you won't go through trials, but God may bless you with favor. God places His children along your path of life to bring glory to Himself and to reveal Himself to people. Don't grow tired of spreading the gospel of Jesus Christ or your testimony around in the world! Stand firm for God Almighty and Jesus Christ!

Chapter 26 Share how God transformed your life from the beginning. You decide if you want to share that God gave you a vision or a word (prophecy). God is the Author of your faith so He writes incredible stories about how He changed you! You never know how being willing to share, being open and honest can help people to develop their relationship with God and Jesus!

Chapter 27 Many people think that they have life "figured" out so they don't listen to God. Life storms rage on and become worse. Some people trust God and are comforted through His Holy Spirit. Others make snap decisions that won't solve anything and may cause greater damage. Life storms don't have a time limit so they can rage for quite awhile. Through them, some people's faith in God becomes stronger and is strengthen! Trust God and He'll keep you safe!

Chapter 28 Lend a helping hand to others while displaying God's love and kindness. If you know that you're God's child, you know that God will protect you from harm through His Holy Spirit. It's time to step out of your comfort zone and go to people to pray for them by joining hands, touching their arm or back. When you thought that your good reputation was ruined because of others' remarks, don't fret because God can avoid those remarks from reaching people. You need to love, be bold, and do not doubt when you share the Word of God (Bible) with others!

End of <u>Acts</u>

Chapter By Chapter

<u>Romans</u>

Chapter 1 When you are confident in sharing your faith in God Almighty, Jesus Christ, and Holy Spirit, you enjoy sharing and become an encourager to others. When people share their faith with you it often strengthens your faith. We have the free choice to believe in God Almighty, Jesus Christ, and Holy Spirit or not to believe in Him. God doesn't force us to have a loving relationship with Him. We can choose to ignore God and disobey His commands. Being a homosexual is wrong. Read Romans 1:26-32 about sinful humanity. The world's actions are mentioned and society is displayed to a tee.

Chapter 2 It's easy being judgmental. Your actions speak volumes to people so instead of acting horrible, show God's love and kindness to them. You never know when acting merciful and compassionate will do. It may cause people to repent and choose to obey what God says to do and not to do in His Word. Make a change to act how God wants instead of hearing the Word and then not implementing the lessons in your life. Actions and words display what's in your heart. Jesus judges on Judgment Day and there's no favoritism so it's either Heaven or the Lake of Fire.

Chapter 3 Your words and actions display the kind of person that you are. Do you curse? Do you speak about your bitterness? You may have a miserable life because of the choices that you have made. Everyone, yes even you, will be judged by Jesus. Your conscious is what you will be judged by if you don't have faith in God, Jesus, and Holy Spirit. Repent of your sins. God is faithful when you're not. Jesus Christ died a brutal death on the cross for you and if you have faith in Him, you are made perfect. You will be judged by the Word of God (Bible).

Chapter 4 You know when you are obeying and living for God or not. I challenge you to examine your life to see if what you are doing is for God or for your own desires. When you act how God wants you to according to His Word and Holy Spirit, you are obedient, rightly standing, and rightly living with God. You need to trust God because life is unpredictable, but with God all things are possible! Just when you don't see the positive in a situation, you should pray and trust God. Don't give up living out your faith when the odds are against you. Believe, trust, obey, and pray to God!

Chapter 5 During trials, try to avoid focusing on the problem. Instead, you should be focusing on praying to God and trusting Him. God molds you and during trials, God is molding your perseverance, character, hope, and His love. Your faith and love for God, Jesus, and Holy Spirit should grow intimate once you grasp a nugget of understanding of what Christ's death means! Jesus saves your soul when you believe in Him!

Chapter 6 How you want to live is your choice. You can live in the party scene and think that it is what satisfies you. When you are born again and are baptized in Christ Jesus your Lord and Savior, you're set free from bondages and chains. You have to believe, trust, and obey God your Father. Baptism means you are declaring you are done following the authority of drugs and other addictions. You are deciding to obey God Almighty, Jesus Christ, and Holy Spirit in life. You are deciding to love, forgive, pray, and lend a helping hand in life.

Chapter 7 You are battling against your soul and flesh if you are choosing to live life in obedience to God in accordance to His Word (Bible). Once you understand His Word, hopefully, you will know what pleases and displeases God. Take His Word to heart and apply the principles to your daily life. When you fail, ask for forgiveness by praying to God and move forward. Your soul will overpower your flesh, as your obedience to God and Holy Spirit grows as you choose to journey in life through Him! Don't give up!

Chapter 8 Ponder about two people with different backgrounds. One person could be into drugs, sleeping around with people, and alcohol. The other person could be into building a relationship with Father God, lending a helping hand to people, and praying about all circumstances. It's your decision whether to live a chaotic and destructive life when reaching for success isn't enough or to live hopeful and peaceful doing God's will. There's nothing that can separate you from the love of God! Endure sufferings for God's glory!

Chapter 9 We all have had moments in our lives that we were striving and straining to reach a goal with our own strength. God allows us to have our freedom to choose to trust and rely on Him through life or to do life by ourselves. Things in life don't and won't make sense unless God reveals His purpose to us, but often we don't understand. God has a plan and it will be completed. Do you believe or have unbelief? God's power and Name will be known in all of the earth either through His mercy or wrath. Right living and right standing with God (righteousness) comes by faith, not pointless traditions that are not from the heart.

Chapter 10 Faith is believing in your Lord Jesus Christ. Pray to God about anything and everything. Read as well as study the Word of God (Bible) and listen to praise and worship music. When you seek God, He will be found and you will get to know Him intimately. Once you spend time with God, Jesus, and Holy Spirit, His Word and characteristics will be display through you! I think when God's children share their faith with others is beautiful. You are Christ's example of who God is in the world.

Chapter 11 Believing in the Lord Jesus Christ means that you are trusting God to nurture you in life. Imagine a tree. It needs water, sun, and roots for growth. God is the root as well as the tree and people are the branches. Praying to God for yourself and others, forgiving, loving, showing gratefulness, and kindness are some aspects that you should have as your characteristics if you say you have faith in God Almighty. When you have unbelief, God will cut you off from Himself (tree) because you are choosing to live and take control of your life. The fruits of the Spirit are love, joy, peace, patience, kindness, goodness, gentleness, faithfulness, and self-control. Act out these nine fruits in life; you may be the person who God uses in order for a loved one to abandon his or her soul to Him. Help God graft in people to His kingdom!

Chapter 12 If you live wholeheartedly for Jesus Christ, you know what you should do to please Him. God blesses His children with gifts, such as prophesying, serving, teaching, being encouraging, giving, lending, and being merciful. Your heart needs to be in the right motive to share. Don't share your gifts out of obligation or tradition; share them because you want to and because you love God! Honor your Lord with excited determination to serve Him by spreading the hope, joy in God with others, being patient in affliction (suffering), praying faithfully, helping the needy, and practicing hospitality. When people are mistreating or are upset with you, pray blessings over them to God and treat them kindly by helping them. Trust God to create a positive outcome that glorifies Him out of the negative situation, but remember to be patient!

Chapter 13 God established authority so you better obey the authorities. Rebelling against them is rebelling against God. Fear and respect mean that you want to do what's correct and have a clean conscience. If you don't respect authority, your wrongdoing will result in punishment. Pay your dues in whatever sort of fashion that may be in, such as taxes, revenue, respect, honor, and etc. But love unconditionally! Jesus is coming back for His children so every moment you are closer to seeing Him face-to-face! Read Romans 13:13 of how not to act if you are truly, not a phony, God's child.

Chapter 14 I need to not pass judgment on others. There's a time for correction and trying to lend a helping hand, but also, a time of letting go. You have to live life the way you know what's rightly standing and rightly living for God. It's your choice whether or not to honor God with your life. If you know someone struggles with something and you tease them about or with it; that's not okay. Help this person with it or avoid it if at all possible. Avoid judging and if you want to, live life-glorifying God! Trust and obey the Holy Spirit because you are accountable for your life and yours alone.

Chapter 15 Life is hard, but you should endure it. Pray to God and share life's moments with others so that they can pray, rejoice, and mourn with you. As God's children reading and studying the Bible should be at times convicting (needing to change) but also, encouraging. God, Jesus, and Holy Spirit is our role model on how we should act in life. When we fail, God gives His grace, mercy, and compassion upon us. We should be acting out His characteristics toward others; teaching the ways of Jesus.

Chapter 16 Now is the time to help people with whatever need you see fit. It's scary and nerve-racking, but through the Holy Spirit, God equips you for the task to fulfill the need. Treat people with God's unconditional love, gentleness, kindness, and humility. You should know when to stand up for your beliefs so that you won't be dismayed. Don't let people put obstacles in your beliefs. Seek God by praying and reading the Bible to know Him!

End of <u>Romans</u>

Chapter By Chapter

1 Corinthians

Chapter 1 Often, actions reveal the kind of person you are. Knowledge and speech are other aspects that can define you. I challenge you to read, study the Bible, and pray to Father God to know how He expects His children to live daily life. As you continue doing this, His Holy Spirit will teach and remind you the ways of God. You should strive to intimately know God to act and talk like Him in the world. What sounds foolish is wise in God's eyes in accordance to His Word (Bible). Boast (speaking proudly) in the Lord, for your faith and strength are in Him!

Chapter 2 Failures are roadblocks that you often can't move pass. You just have to be yourself and obedient to God's authority. His power and glory will shine forth so continue praising Him in life. Ask God for wisdom to know how He wants you to handle situations. God's Holy Spirit teaches and helps you understand spiritual mysteries that the wise people on earth can't comprehend. With a humble heart and empty hands, God can do extraordinary miracles through you! Be confident in your Lord and be like He is in your world!

Chapter 3 Jealousy and quarreling ruin many relationships. You should love one another and be content with your life at its present state. Stop comparing your life with another's. Grow in love with God so you can scatter seeds (gospel) and water the seeds so that God can make them grow! You scatter seeds by your actions and water seeds by explaining the Word of God to others. Build a firm foundation in Christ by praying to God with a sincere heart, reading the Bible, asking questions, listening to sermons, and worship songs (Christian songs). Be diligent in building your foundation in Christ so you can withstand trials in this life, but also stand firm on Judgment Day! Don't be deceived; obey and trust God in all things! Remember what seems foolish is wise in God's eyes in accordance to His Word (Bible).

Chapter 4 We are too quick to judge others. There are times where we need to correct by the Word of God. But we should be conscious about living for Father God; pleasing Him, not people. Jesus is the One and only Judge who will judge everyone. We should be striving to know God intimately to help spread the gospel around the world. Knowing and living for Christ is wise. Yet people think we're fools. "When we are cursed, we bless; when we are persecuted, we endure it; when we are slandered, we answer kindly." (1 Corinthians 4:12-13) If you are not acting this way in life in accordance to 1 Corinthians 4:12-13, begin from this moment on! Faithfully live before God Almighty and act like Him because He entrusts His Word to you! Spread and explain His Word to others. God's kingdom is real and powerful!

Chapter 5 We have opinions on what is right and what is wrong. We have to decide if we will help the immoral people by praying but also, inviting them to church. There's power in our Lord's presence! It's to loosen people from their chains of bondage and free them in Christ! Throw away and be done with your immoral habits. Establish an intimate relationship with your Lord Jesus Christ! Be God's spokesperson in the world and avoid spending time with the sexually immoral, greedy, idolater, slander, drunker, or a swindler. Don't let their habits become yours. We want them to seek God and be done with their sinful destructive habits.

Chapter 6 People become upset over the slightest things and they want the authorities to settle the dispute. As God's children, we should pray to seek God's guidance, trust Him, and then ask for the authorities to help. We should be reading and studying the Bible daily because the world is getting worse. It's difficult to know right from wrong because many people are just accepting the evil practices because they are coming the norm. It's time to take a stand to grow your relationship with God and to display His forgiving, loving, and kindness characteristics. Again don't associate with a sexually immoral, greedy, idolater, slander, drunker, or a swindler. Be determined to just say, "No" to people! "Do you not know that your bodies are temples of the Holy Spirit, who is in you, whom you have received from God? You are not your own; you were bought at a price. Therefore honor God with your bodies." (1 Corinthians 6:19-20)

Chapter 7 You have to make the decision on how to live your life. There are times where you should seek guidance. What works for someone's life may not work for another's. You should pray to Father God and be obedient to Him. God has a purpose for you so study the Bible to know Him. You have desires that are different from your loved ones and you need to take responsibility for them so that you won't be tormented. Focus on worshiping God and aim to serve Him with a hot passion! He will bless you abundantly if you seek Him first and wholeheartedly!

Chapter 8 People make mistakes and choices occur on how to deal with them. Often people will be judgmental and say snooty remarks. Instead of acting this way, say encouraging words, love on people, and help them. This helps with building self-esteems. If you're a follower of Christ, display that truth by your daily actions. Out of your love for God, respectfully fear Father God, promptly obeying Him by His Holy Spirit, and intimately knowing God is a treasure; act this out in your daily life! Be conscious about your actions and words because they can be encouraging, damaging or a stumbling block to people. You should be displaying God's love in the world, not wanting people to fail.

Chapter 9 God may use you to spread His gospel around in your life. Pray to God to ask for His wisdom to share His Word. You know when it's time to share the gospel. Be bold and confident. Plus being persecuted for Jesus Christ is joyful. You should be friendly to people and help them out, but remember to share the gospel. You will be judged, but your focus should be on pleasing God and spreading hope, joy, and peace that are in Him! You have to have the desire to intimately know Him and self-discipline to read His Word (Bible) daily plus live it out. Remember to freely give your time and energy because God loves you and Jesus was crucified for you; freely receive! Desire to save souls for Father God!

Chapter 10 You are either serving, honoring, following, relying on God wholeheartedly; desiring to know Him more or you are living life as you please. The Word of God says Father Almighty is a jealous God and don't test God. You should give God your undivided attention; always trusting Him even in the trials. "No temptation has overtaken you except what is common to mankind. And God is faithful; he will not let you be tempted beyond what you can bear. But when you are tempted, he will also provide a way out so that you can endure it." (1 Corinthians 10:13) So remember to be conscious about your actions and words because they can be encouraging, damaging or a stumbling block to people. You should be displaying God's love in the world, not wanting people to fail. Let God glorify Himself through your daily life!

Chapter 11 It's easy to serve God and people when life occurs smoothly, but when life seems like a raging storm serving can be difficult. God created authority so everything is under His authority! We have to submit to authority if it lines up with God's Word. Take care of one another by putting their needs before yours. It's time to encourage people and practice daily the Word of God in life seriously! Examine your heart; repent by praying to God, and desire to change for God's glory! Remember change takes time and effort so be patient.

Chapter 12 In Christ, we are many parts and have different strengths of His nine spiritual gifts. These nine gifts if used properly, are to serve and glorify Father God. These gifts are a message of wisdom (speaking the word that's from God), a message of knowledge (expressing and giving understanding to the word), faith, gifts of healing, miraculous powers, prophecy, distinguishing of spirits, and the interpretation of spirits. God blesses us with these as He determines! His Holy Spirit is for everyone! With sincerity in your heart, ask God for His Holy Spirit to dwell within you, helping you learn God's ways so you can rightly live out and spread His gospel around. "But in fact God has placed the parts in the body, every one of them, just as he wanted them to be." (1 Corinthians 12:18) Humbly do your job; honoring God!

Chapter 13 You should help out others whether that is using the nine spiritual gifts of God's Holy Spirit or being hospitable even if it's blessing them with the essentials. But helping doesn't mean anything if God's love isn't penetrating through your actions onto others. Read 1 Corinthians 13:4-8 in the Amplified Bible because it gives in-depth detail on love rather than hearing it in church or at weddings. As a child of God, you understand and think in part because of sin that came in the world in the beginning. When Jesus comes back to earth, everything will be created to be perfect; the true reality as God intended it for! Deepen your faith in Father God, hope in Him, and love! Love unconditionally!

Chapter 14 When you speak in tongues, you are speaking to Father God and encouraging yourself. Prophecies encourage the church. You should be conscious how you use these gifts and if there's someone to interpret, be confident in speaking because the message will be spoken. Pray to God with your voice and speaking in tongues. God may use you to lead people to Him and start a relationship with Him. God instructs the church good orders to worship. Examine them for yourselves.

Chapter 15 Grace is an undeserved act of kindness beyond what God's children deserve and is a blessing from our Almighty God! We live on earth in an imperfect body. We, as Father God's children, daily have to battle with ourselves to avoid being selfish and acting carelessly. Each second is a moment we can choose to believe in God Almighty, trust Him, act His Word (Bible) out, or to be ignorant. Remember 1 Corinthians 15:33 says, ""Do not be misled: "Bad company corrupts good character."" Decide to believe in the Lord Jesus

Christ because once your body stops functioning, your soul lives forever in God's kingdom! Everything changes in the blink of an eye so complete your Lord's work with enthusiasm because of your love for Father God!

Chapter 16 Set a goal to bless others by deliberately having a budgeting envelope and be determined to set a sum of money weekly or monthly so you can bless others. If your mind is set on growing your relationship with Father God and helping people, your problems seem inadequate. It's time to be an encourager and to share the gospel with people! Always read and study the Bible, and pray to God Almighty earnestly! Be on your guard, stand firm in your faith, and always love people every second of the day!

End of <u>1 Corinthians</u>

2 Corinthians

Chapter 1 Cling to and rely on Father God. He is compassionate and comforts us. As our relationship with Him grows, we experience His compassion and comfort; realizing that Father God is whom we should depend on. Hopefully, when our faith is firm, we are able to help others in their trials by praying for them and sharing God's wisdom. Don't act as if you care for the moment, then the next, you gossip. You should be a person who is loyal. With love and patience, empathize with one another: sharing in the rejoicing and suffering moments.

Chapter 2 It's easy to grieve or become annoyed with people when they hurt you in some sort of way. You can hang this hurt over their heads or choose to pray for them: asking for help to forgive them, blessing them, and positively encourage them. Satan hates God's children when they are actively living out and performing the Word of God (Bible) out in everyday life. So keep on loving, forgiving, and studying and doing God's Word! Be diligent in knowing Father God so that He will bless you with opportunities to share His gospel with others. If you wholeheartedly love and are in love with God, you should fragrance the world in Christ Jesus by acting merciful and compassionate. Remember His aroma is sweet, peaceful, and is life to others, but for others, His aroma is death. Speak of Father God with a sincerity and purest motive with others! Always pray!

Chapter 3 You should desire to know Father God intimately and actively live out the Bible. In life, you should want to honor and praise God Almighty because you know, through His Holy Spirit; God has the power to do anything. Be humble, bold, and confident before God's throne and in life. Where the Spirit of the Lord is, there is freedom! In Christ, you enjoy life because you are in love with Him, getting to know Him, and blessing others through His Spirit. Strip off your bondages that are chaining you, surrender your soul and control of your life to our Lord Jesus Christ because He satisfies you; makes you whole! As you continue your faith relationship, God's glory will radiant through your life and will be a love letter; known and read by everyone!

Chapter 4 When you are in a loving and respectful relationship with Father God, you have a desire to explain the Truth and are hurt when God is misrepresented. You are saddened to see people struggling because you know who God is and that He takes care of you. You are in a raging war because the world doesn't understand whom God, Jesus, Holy Spirit is. Jesus is the Way, the Truth, and the Life; nothing is hidden from Him. Since the world doesn't understand "we are hard pressed on every side, but not crushed; perplexed, but not in despair; persecuted, but not abandoned; struck down, but not destroyed. We always carry around in our body the death of Jesus, so that the life of Jesus may also be revealed in our body." (2 Corinthians 4:8-10) Persecution for Jesus Christ is worth enduring because you will see the glory of God in His entire splendor! "So we fix our eyes not on what is seen, but on what is unseen, since what is seen is temporary, but what is unseen is eternal." (2 Corinthians 4:18)

Chapter 5 Some people are longing for Heaven because on earth people are groaning and burdensome in this immoral life. People, we all will be judged on how we lived our lives, whether good or bad by Jesus Christ. We, who love Christ with our whole being, should be acting and speaking out His Word (Bible). Pray to Father God, study, practice His Word in life, and share His Word with others. Also, share your testimony because God may use it to soften hearts. It may help people desire to surrender their souls to Him and live life that's pleasing to Him; God Almighty.

Chapter 6 Prepare to be a spokesperson for Almighty God at any given moment. We should be willing to spend time loving people who are in need. Helping and being positive are encouragers to people. You should share God's wisdom every chance you get, but do it lovingly. Remember you are Father God's representative so share who He is to people! Influence them to know and love God sincerely!

Chapter 7 Corrections need to be made on a regular bases. Change is a process so be patient. You often don't want to hear the harsh comments or the truth, but when you pray to God;

asking for guidance; it may change your eternal address. Asking God for forgiveness of your wrongs and desiring to act like how Father God tells you to act according to the Bible brings joy in life! Knowing who God is gives you confidence to live for His glory!

Chapter 8 Share your faith, love, and knowledge of the gospel with people at any given moment. Your passion for Father God should be overflowing outside of you. During trials is when your faith is tested all the more. Loving, being kind, and having generosity can be difficult. Through the trials and the pain, don't stop trusting God. Keep praying to Father God, studying and implementing what His Word says in life. Love Almighty God and people more as well as have generosity beyond your comfort zone. God will supply for your needs if you honor and trust Him with everything in life!

Chapter 9 When you give to others, you shouldn't give reluctantly or give at the spur of the moment. You should give generously from your heart, praying about it. You decide how much that you want to give and depending on your love for Father God, faith, and trust in Him, He will bless you. Share your passion and enthusiasm for God because you may be leading people to Christ! Love, care, and give grace to others according to God's Word so that Father God can bless people through your life! Be a person who people pray for and praise

God for because of your actions display how to live according to God's Word (Bible).

Chapter 10 Read Ephesians 6:14-18 for knowledge of the weapons that Father God has blessed you with to live on this earth. Remember to display God's unconditional love, kindness, gentleness, goodness, peace, patience, and joy to people. Life is hard and so, will you share the gospel with people and continue acting the way you know is pleasing to Father God? Quit comparing yourself to others and start living according to God's Word (Bible). You can make a difference when your relationship with Christ is rock solid.

Chapter 11 We, the Church are the Bride of Christ. We should be eager to please Father God because He loves us and we love Him. Share the gospel and your testimony with others to give honor to our God. Tell about your weaknesses, pains, and trials in which Father God has brought you through: lavishing His great glory, love, and power on you. Be aware of false teaching; twisting the truth of the message of the gospel. Be active, alert, and attentive to knowing God's Word plus acting the Word out because when you least expect it, you may be deceived. Father God will punish the false teachers according to what their actions deserve.

Chapter 12 Often you don't speak of your weaknesses, pains, or trials because of embarrassment and judgmental reasons. Christ's power is unleashed in your weakness. In your weaknesses, insults, hardships, persecutions, and difficulties, share how your Lord brought you through and made you stronger. Love people as Father God and Christ love His Bride, the Church! He provides for you. I know loving your enemies is easier said then done. But God equips you to love them if you sincerely pray to Him about it. Sharing your weaknesses gives Father God glory and can strengthen others on their spiritual journey. So what if you are humiliated. You should be humbled before God Almighty!

Chapter 13 You are the only person who knows if you are living for Christ; obeying Him, and applying His Word in your life. Examine your faith journey with God. Strive to be Christ-like!

End of 2 Corinthians

Chapter By Chapter

<u>Galatians</u>

Chapter 1 You have to decide to be fully dependent on Father God! Make a determined effort to read, study, and believe the gospel of your Lord Jesus Christ. God breathed His Word (Bible) for your benefit and is a tool that you are blessed to have. You decide when you are quitting being a people-pleaser and allowing life to toss you in the wind. You need to choose that you fully and completely with all that you are, desire to live life with the purpose of pleasing and honoring Father God. Strive to spend time with Father God daily and He will begin to mold you into His image. God has a purpose for you and all that you have to do is give up the control in your life and decide to follow Father God's lead in whatever fashion that looks like. Just trust God because the life journey is amazing!

Chapter 2 You have to have the desire to grow your intimate relationship with Father God. Read His Word (Bible) and pray to God by sharing what's on your heart. Your desire should be to know and be in love with Father God that you share His characteristics with everyone. When something is incorrect with people portraying the gospel of Lord Jesus Christ, you are the one who needs to stand up and correct them. Christ died for you so why not help God lavish His love on people so that He can lead them into a life that's fulfilling!

Chapter 3 Faith comes from hearing and believing in the gospel of Lord Jesus Christ. The belief and the constant continuation of doing what God's Word (Bible) says to do and what not to do are what God desires you to have in your faith relationship with Him. You should know that apart from God you have nothing and life is meaningless. But when you choose to live for Christ and are baptized into His Name, you are set free from practicing man-made traditions. Jesus died for you so you can pray to Father God without having a mediator praying for you. Chapter 4 When you are not of age to make decisions on your own, you have to obey the authority figures who are in your life. You are tossed around in the middle of chaos, but when you choose to believe in and form an intimate relationship with God, you are relying on God to fully take care of you in life. People will try to pull you away from worshipping and serving God; Jesus Christ your Savior. You may not notice this immediately, but just build your relationship with God by reading the Bible and praying to God daily. You are God's child because you believe in Jesus and the power of His death! You have to live by faith and not let bad influences rob you from obeying God. Love, but stand firm in who you believe in! Chapter 5 Express why you are in love with God, sharing how much He has blessed you with, and the gospel with others. You don't need to live life according to Galatians 5:19-21. If you want to have a serious relationship with Father God, then be serious in seeking Him. He will teach you love, joy, peace, patience, goodness, kindness, faithfulness, gentleness, and self-control. Be careful on how you live because you may be deceived. Pray to God about everything. Through His Holy Spirit, God will guide you in life!

Christ Jesus died for you so you can live life free. You are allowed to live free from strict rules, but remember, when you obey the authority figures, you are obeying God Himself. God desires your whole being to be committed to worshipping, serving, and following Him in every season of life. It's time to give up the control, hand it to Father God, and not let others toss you around in life. Build up your faith relationship with Father God by studying the Bible and praying with a 100 percent heart devotion. You are in a war against your flesh and God's Holy Spirit in living life. Study the gospel and act like Father God in everyday life!

Chapter 6 When you have an intimate relationship with Father God, Jesus Christ, and Holy Spirit, you should know what pleases and displeases God Almighty. So be determined to act like Christ in all of life's circumstances. Remember, how you act will result in destruction or you will have eternal life. Stand firm in Christ Jesus and live life honoring God. Share the gospel with everyone and do good in all things! Seek God on how to live life, not others!

End of <u>Galatians</u>

Ephesians

Chapter 1 You just have to believe in Jesus Christ in your heart and be unashamed when you speak of Him to people. Personalize Jesus Christ's life, death, and resurrection for you; He did it for you out of His great love for you to give you every spiritual blessing in life. He has formed you for a purpose in life. You must be willing to receive His wisdom and understanding with a pure and soften-heart devoted to God your Father, Jesus Christ, and Holy Spirit. Do things for God because you love Him, His people, and have faith in Lord Jesus Christ. You are God's child so share with others what He has blessed you with!

Chapter 2 You don't have to act like everyone else. You can choose to be different. Choose to live life by faith in the Son of God and not be a partaker in acting evil. God's gracious act of kindness and blessing gave you a gift of the Holy Spirit. It's time to get rid of the stereotypical nametags that you put on people and start having harmony in our unity when we meet together. Christ built His Church so we should be representing Him well because we are His Church!

Chapter 3 The Holy Spirit gives God's children the power and authority to understand the gospel of Jesus Christ. You have the freedom to through faith boldly, confidently, but in humility, pray to Father God whatever is on your heart. There's supposed to be unity in the Church, in which we share with each other our joys as well as trials. You are God's chosen one so depending on God, you may be the one who He chooses to use in order for people to understand and believe in Him. Grasp how unconditional God's love is for you and you are blessed to speak to Him about everything whenever! Once you grasp a nugget of that, your mind will be blown away! Because of God's great love for you, He will bless you far beyond what you can imagine!

Chapter 4 You should be humble, gentle, patient, and loving people through every season of life. Share the gospel like you know how because someday soon Father God will reveal all things of Christ that you understand a small-fraction of. You won't be tossed in the wind of this chaotic world because God will mature your faith relationship with Him so you can stop living life as you once did, to begin living life that honors God. Be done with revenge and start loving, forgiving, and being merciful to others! Lend your time in helping others to live life pleasing to God. Keep unity and harmony in your life with everyone!

Chapter 5 God loves you so much that He made Jesus to be human and come down on earth to show you how to live life that's pleasing to Him. Then Jesus died a brutal death for you. He didn't bad talk anyone or anything. Jesus wasn't selfish; just always loved and cared for others. It's time to share the good news and the truth of the gospel with everyone. When you know God and how much He loves you, you can love yourself and others like Christ. You can decide how to act; bitter or peaceful because of your love for God!

Chapter 6 The way you act and treat others is very important, so if you want Father God to bless you, do everything for His glory. Remember Father God doesn't show favoritism so He will reward you based upon your heart and life you lived. God blessed you with armor because He knew that living in this world would be tough. Evil is raging war against the spiritual realms. So you are in a battle every second of everyday if you wholeheartedly believe in God, Jesus, and Holy Spirit. You have to stand up and stand firm in sharing the truth of the gospel of Jesus Christ. Even when nobody else is behaving himself or herself according to the Word of God, you should be behaving yourself with integrity because you know full well what's pleasing to God. You need to be ready and on top of your game to share the gospel at the spur of the moment at any given moment. Speak out the Word of God in life and pray to God about every detail in your life because that's how intimate Father God desires your relationship to be with Him!

End of <u>Ephesians</u>

Chapter By Chapter

Philippians

Chapter 1 When you believe in and intimately know Father God, He will bless you with a caring-heart and knowledge of understanding in spreading the gospel of Lord Jesus Christ around to people. God blesses you with boldness and confidence to rely on Him in life because you know that His plan for your life is the best and He will bring it into completion if you diligently seek Him with your whole being. You will face persecution and opposition because of your faith in Jesus Christ. So spread your faith in Jesus Christ around everywhere in your life! So what if you face persecution and opposition. Your desire should be for everyone to know Father God, Jesus, and Holy Spirit. Live for Christ and spread God's Word around by actively living it in your daily life!

Chapter 2 Share encouragement, comfort, love, tenderness, and compassion that you have received from Jesus Christ with others so that they too can be loved. When you have a relationship with God, Jesus, and Holy Spirit, He molds your heart to think of and put others' needs before your own. So in humility, serve one another in any kind of way because you are in love with Jesus. Don't be a two-faced kind of person who acts sweet and caring one minute, but in the next, is grumbling and complaining. That's not how Father God wants you to act if you are truly His child. You must be so in love with God, Jesus, and

Holy Spirit that you would die for the sake of spreading the gospel for others to choose Jesus as their Lord and Savior!

Chapter 3 Once you have an intimate relationship with Father God, know the power of Jesus Christ's resurrection, and His gift of Holy Spirit, you will understand that what the world offers or entices you with is worthless. A popular name, where your birthplace was, your work environment, and things you enjoy doing are meaningless when you aren't honoring God with your life. You should be striving to share what God has done for you in your life with others to help them realize that clinging to and relying on Father God is the answer in overcoming as well as living peaceably on this earth!

Chapter 4 Praying is so important that you should view it as breathing. It doesn't matter what or where you are, pray just as long as you are praying to Father God. You should know how to act, in which honors God in all circumstances. Allow God to mold and mature you through His Holy Spirit so that you know how to be content in all seasons of life. Focus on how much God has blessed you with and praising Him! Why not share and bless others with what God has blessed you with because He provides for your needs if you trust Him.

End of <u>Philippians</u>

Chapter By Chapter

<u>Colossians</u>

Chapter 1 When you have faith in your Lord Jesus Christ, through His Holy Spirit, Father God molds your heart to deepen your faith relationship and love for Him as well a love for others. If you are sincere, pray and ask Father God for more of His knowledge, wisdom, and understanding to live life that is pleasing to Him. You should strive to act like Christ according to the gospel because God produces the good fruit in you, the knowledge of God grows, and you are strengthened in power so that you are blessed with endurance and patience. Share your joyful thanks that you are God's child with others! Don't ever let your hope in your Lord or zeal be snuffed out!

Chapter 2 People enjoy being encouraged so you should share with others from a pure heart and with love the mysteries of Christ with wisdom and understanding that Father God has blessed you with. You should stand up and share your beliefs with others. Don't be deceive or conform to the world's surroundings. You have to live life the way that the Holy Spirit guides you.

Chapter 3 Make the decision to be fully determined to live life that's worthy of God and spreading the gospel of Lord Jesus Christ. Don't be entangled in the traps of sexual immorality, impurity, lust, evil desires, or greed. God desires you to act compassionate, kind, humble, gentle, and have patience with others. You need to be involved with people so you can rejoice when they are rejoicing, mourn when they are mourning, but most importantly, always love. Forgive others as your Lord forgave you. Speak encouraging words and share the wisdom of the gospel with everyone! Be obedient to the Holy Spirit and live life in respect to God!

Chapter 4 Ask Father God to strengthen your faith in Him so that you know how to bless people by loving and providing for their needs. You need to be always ready to share the gospel of your Lord Jesus Christ, His wisdom and teaching no matter if the conversation is about God or not; be ready to share God's message with everyone! Standing firm in the will of God is applying God's Word (Bible) in your daily life through all of the seasons of life and through God's Holy Spirit, God will mature your faith in the Deity, which is God the Father, Christ the Son, and Holy Spirit! As your faith grows, you should be confident in the Lord!

End of <u>Colossians</u>

1 Thessalonians

Chapter 1 Act out your faith that is powered by the Holy Spirit. Your faith in God should overflow out of you in love and helping others. Endure the trials and don't ever let them quench your hope that you have in Lord Jesus Christ. You need to embrace the change that Father God is confronting you about through His gospel and other motives. Do away with idols so you can serve the living and true God whose mighty to save!

Chapter 2 You need to be encouraging, comforting, and urging people to live life for the glory of God. Share your mountaintop stories about how Father God blessed you as well as your trials and opposition that you have faced. This will help others on their faith journey with Lord Jesus Christ. Share God's gospel so that people can live life that's holy, blameless, and fully entrusted in the Lord!

Chapter 3 Your faith in Lord Jesus Christ will be tested and you will be persecuted. It's important to know how to strengthen and encourage yourself in your faith. Sing onto the Lord a new song, praise God, and think of God's Word continually. The Holy Spirit will bring forth Scriptures to help you on your faith and love journey with God so you can act like Him in your daily life! Stand firm in Lord Jesus Christ and share His gospel with others so that their faith can grow! Make God proud of you so that when Jesus comes back He's proud to call you His son or daughter!

Chapter 4 Often the unspoken words and the constant steadiness are what people need to see in you so that Father God can reveal Himself to them. Now is the time to live a quiet and simple life: always willing to lend a helping hand to others. Fully and wholeheartedly depend on Father God, Jesus Christ, and Holy Spirit in life to gain respect, but also to show that God is real! Someday and one day soon, Jesus is coming back with everyone who have faith in Him and the people who have chosen to live for Lord Jesus Christ living on earth will be united with Christ and have eternal life forever! So don't grieve, but rejoice and share the gospel of Lord Jesus Christ with everyone!

Chapter 5 Daily put on faith in Lord Jesus Christ and God's love as a breastplate as well as the hope of salvation as a helmet. Be always ready to share what God has blessed you with others. Encourage, help the weak, be patient with everyone, and act in God's love. Give respect to everyone who God used in building and strengthening your faith in Him. Sometimes God may use you to strengthen their faith in return. Don't pay back evil for evil. Pray to Father God about everything so that He can mold you into His image! Jesus Christ is coming back on earth soon so share His gospel and characteristics with everyone!

End of <u>1 Thessalonians</u>

Chapter By Chapter

2 Thessalonians

Chapter 1 Ask Father God in prayer to increase and deepen your faith in Him more and more each day that He blesses you with on earth. Love others like God loves you; being compassionate, merciful, and gracious to them when all they are doing is evil. If you desire to be leaning your whole personality on God in absolute trust and confidence in His power, wisdom, and goodness, you will have trials and be faced with persecutions because of your faith in Lord Jesus Christ. Endure the trials and persecutions because Father God fights for you when your actions and heart are solely devoted to honor Him in everything in life!

Chapter 2 The world is getting more and more evil. Morals are being erased, in which people don't know right from wrong. Satan's evil spirits are destroying everything and deceiving people from hearing as well as living out the truth of the gospel of Lord Jesus Christ. God has given you the free choice whether or not to follow Him in life or go on your own way. Apply God's wisdom, understanding, and teaching to your life to stand firm in faith!

Chapter 3 When you feel as if you are spiritually lacking, pray to God for His unending love to be lavish upon you, His strength, and perseverance. Pray that God will use you by not only put His gospel into action in daily life, but to honor your Lord Jesus Christ by sharing His message with people. If you say that you are truly God's child, you have to want to love, be merciful, and help others. It's no good to be in many activities and not want to grow your relationship with God. Check your motives and there may be a time for a change. If you want God to protect you, seek Him with all that you are by relying on Him to lead you through life! Don't stop doing what is good in God's eyes and He will bless you with His peace!

End of <u>2 Thessalonians</u>

1 Timothy

Chapter 1 Do you have a pure heart that is solely devoted to and in love with Father God, Jesus Christ, and Holy Spirit? Along with your pure heart, you should have a good conscience, and a sincere faith to rightly live before God. Father God lavishes undeserved kindness and blesses you with blessings because of His great love for you! Share what God has blessed you with, with others; don't share if you want to have self-seeking praises from people. You won't be blessed and your life will crumble down on you. Hold onto your faith and a good conscience before God so that He can receive the glory that He deserves in your life!

Chapter 2 Pray to Father God about anything and everything. Pour out your deepest heart cry that is brewing inside. Father God is always there waiting for you to talk to Him, but someday soon it will be too late if you just call out to God in the day of distress. Your heart should be on fire with a hot passion for God now; knowing and learning His knowledge of the truth, then acting them out in life. Pray about everything and obey the guidance of the Holy Spirit because the Lord will direct your steps if you wholeheartedly live for God! So build your faith and love with God to live life that honors Him!

Chapter 3 Father God desires you to act faithful, self-controlled, respectable, hospitable, able to teach, and gentle. Don't become tangled up in the gossip or drama trap because it's pointless and no good will come from it. It can corrupt your good morals. How you act and once people have a friendship with you, then they will know if you are trustworthy or not. Act in respect to Father God; not being a drunk, not violent, or a lover of money. God may use you to bring glory and honor to His Name, but you must be wholeheartedly willing to submit to His authority!

Chapter 4 Reading, studying the Bible, praying to God Almighty the concerns that are on your heart, and applying God's truths to your daily life are what Father God desires you to be. Just like exercising to improve your body, you need to exercise your godliness in building up your spiritual faith journey. Put your hope and trust in the living God; share His gospel with everyone. Desire to intimately know Father God so that your speech, actions, love, faith, and virtue radiate God's compassionate characteristics. Don't allow your age to stop you from sharing the gospel with everyone. It's time to be bold and confident in sharing and living out your beliefs in front of people! Don't give up in standing firm in your beliefs until you see Jesus face-to-face!

Chapter 5 You should make the decision to desire to seek Father God in prayer and with diligence for how to live life that honors Him. You need to set your mind in which your mind, will, and emotions are centered on Jesus Christ in which; all aspects of your life glorify Father God. Out of your on fire love for Lord Jesus Christ, do good deeds by helping others out.

Don't let life pass by and all you did was sat on your duff to gossip. Break out from the chains of Satan and his false reputation of you to start doing good deeds for your Lord! Preach and teach God's gospel to everyone. How you live your life is known by everyone, so why not honor Jesus with it and shine His light in it!

Chapter 6 There are temptations in this world, which can lead you into a sinking ship. If you have faith in God the Father, Jesus Christ the Son, and the Holy Spirit, and have food and clothing, you are blessed and should be content with that in life. "..Pursue righteousness, godliness, faith, love, endurance and gentleness. Fight the good fight of the faith. Take hold of the eternal life to which you were called when you made your good confession in the presence of many witnesses." (1 Timothy 6:11-12) Put your hope in God; cling to, rely upon, and trust in Father God, Holy Spirit for Him to richly provide for your needs to be blessed with an enjoyable life! Continue to submit to God and doing good deeds by helping others. Don't let life pass by and all you did was sat on your duff to gossip. Put into compassionate action your faith and love walk with Lord Jesus Christ in your daily life; everywhere you go!

End of <u>1 Timothy</u>

Chapter By Chapter

2 Timothy

Chapter 1 Ask Father God in prayer to bless you with His gift of the Holy Spirit so you can have God's power, love, self-discipline, and sincere faith. Once Father God ignites this on fire faith and passion for His kingdom's work to be done on earth, don't ever let be burned out. Suffering for Lord Jesus Christ and being persecuted for the sake of the gospel are joys when your faith is sincere!

Chapter 2 You have to know the world's events that are transpiring, but not allow them to consume or control you. Be aware of the world's events, but determined to seek Father God and to share His gospel, the word of truth; continue living life glorifying and unashamed of being a child of God. Stop arguing and gossiping because now is the time to take a stand; not entertaining with wickedness to rise again with Christ Jesus! Endure hardships with Christ Jesus because He is faithful and will make a way out. If you disown and walk from your Lord, He will disown you. He knows who His children are and who have built their solid foundation of faith upon His Name. "Flee the evil desires of youth and pursue righteousness, faith, love and peace, along with those who call on the Lord out of a pure heart." (2 Timothy 2:22)

Chapter 3 I think that there will be a time; much worse than people act now, of people who will be lovers of themselves, lovers of money, boastful, proud, abusive, disobedient to their parents, ungrateful, unholy, without love, unforgiving, not lovers of the good, and fake Christians who deny the power and the truth that are in Christ Jesus. The people who attend church to just warm the pew. They don't learn or apply the knowledge to their own personal everyday lives. It's so important to read and study the Bible for yourself because God will teach, rebuke, correct, and train you how to rightly live for Him by allowing Him to shine His light through you! If you desire to be a fully equipped servant of God, study the Bible and act out the Word to show yourself approved by God and worthy of doing good deeds for His kingdom! Father God teaches you through His Holy Spirit about life, purpose, faith, patience, love, endurance, persecutions, and sufferings in His Word (Bible). You just have to be willing to surrender everything in life over to Father God, pray to Him, trust, cling to Him, and read as well as act out the Bible daily!

Chapter 4 At any given moment, you should be thoroughly ready to speak and share the word of truth; the gospel message of Lord Jesus Christ. Seek Father God for confidence and strength to share His gospel with others in instances for correcting, rebuking, and encouraging, but ask God to bless you with gallons of great patience. You will be persecuted because of your Lord Jesus Christ and for standing firm in your understanding of the gospel. Many people look for others who believe and act the same way as they do. Be determined to be an on fire follower and servant for Lord Jesus Christ. "...Keep your head in all situations, endure hardship, do the work of an evangelist, discharge all the duties of your ministry." (2 Timothy 4:5) God promises that He will never leave or forsake you, so put yourself out there to preach the Word, and God will protect you, if your heart is in love with Him!

End of 2 Timothy

Titus

Chapter 1 It's excellent to have wise God-fearing people who are willing to teach you the knowledge of the truth of the gospel of Lord God Almighty in hopes of you strengthening your faith! How you act and speak tells what kind of person you are. God doesn't want you to act overbearing, quick-tempered, not given to drunkenness, not violent, not pursuing dishonest gain. Rather, he [you] must be hospitable, one who loves what is good, who is self-controlled, upright, holy and disciplined. He {you} must hold firmly to the trustworthy message as it has been taught, so that he {you} can encourage others by sound doctrine and refute those who oppose it (Titus 1:7-9). Don't be someone who claims to know Father God when really, you don't have the slightest clue about who He is. Let your actions and words display God's awesome glory in your life!

Chapter 2 Study the Word of God (Bible) to know whom Father God is, to build your faith relationship, and in doing so, you are able to teach others. Seek Father God by constantly reading His Word, praying to Him, and obeying Him when His Holy Spirit nudges you to do something. When you wholeheartedly do these out of your love for Lord God Almighty, through His Holy Spirit, Father God will equip you to teach others in areas, such as how to be temperate, worthy of respect, self-controlled, sound in faith, in love, and in endurance. God teaches you to say, "No" to ungodly things when you are committed in following Him in life. Be bold and confident when you are encouraging or rebuking others to live pure lives before the throne of God!

Chapter 3 Respect and obey your authority figures; always do what is good, don't create bad reputations for others, be peaceable, considerate, and gentle toward everyone. Don't be foolish, disobedient, deceived, and enslaved by all kinds of passions and pleasures; don't do evil things, don't be envious, or have hatred. God's kindness, love, and mercy are what saved you through Jesus Christ. Jesus gave you His Holy Spirit to display righteousness by blessing you with undeserved act of kindness to become heirs and have the hope of eternal life. Pray to Father God; devote and entrust to Him every aspect in your life so that you can do good things for Father God!

End of Titus

Chapter By Chapter

<u>Philemon</u>

Chapter 1 Strive to be known for your love for God's people and faith in Lord Jesus Christ. You should desire to be effective in deepening your understanding of the gospel and completing good deeds out of your love for Christ. Stand up and firm in your beliefs to continue having the joy of the Lord and to be an encouragement for others. A loved one may have to spend time away from you in order for God to mold and mature him or her. Separation is hard, but if you allow Father God to do His plan and will, the result is glorious! You may be appreciative and have more love to give.

End of <u>Philemon</u>

Hebrews

Chapter 1 God has spoken to us, His children, through His Son Jesus Christ, on how to live life representing Father God's perfect image and glory. Jesus bears the weight of all things by His powerful Word and dying on the cross, but Jesus rose again and is seated by the right-hand-side of Father God in the Heavens. His death makes us clean from sin and free from guilt. God has made Jesus superior over everything and His Name is above all names; there's power in the Name of Jesus! If you consider yourself to be a son or daughter of the Most High God, you should be sharing and living out the gospel all the time to help people know God and enter His kingdom!

Chapter 2 We must be extremely careful in what teachings we listen to about the Word of God (Bible). The message of and the actions of the gospel should be shared with everyone. Jesus Christ was made human so He knows what we are going through because He was tempted so He is able to help us when we are being tempted. If we know how to use the gifts, in which God has blessed us with, we should be spreading the love of Jesus more rapidly in the world! Jesus is our faithful and merciful high priest and paid for our wrongs by dying on the cross so we should strive to act like Him to everyone!

Chapter 3 We should consume and be so consumed with Lord Jesus Christ; thinking about Him and acting like He is every moment that we are blessed living on this earth. Think on heavenly things because Father God is please when our actions and words are confirmed in knowing Christ Jesus. Obey Father God because He is the builder of everything and will bless you abundantly if you believe in Jesus wholeheartedly! Strive to be someone who stands firm in Jesus Christ and encourages others by sharing the gospel or a positive statement.

Chapter 4 Father God says not to worry about what you will eat, drink, or wear for He, your Heavenly Father, knows your needs. You have to keep watch. Guard your words and thoughts because it's easy to be lukewarm in your faith. Pretty soon you are drifting into iceberg city where you have no faith at all in Father God, Jesus Christ, or Holy Spirit. It's time to stop with being consumed with drama and consume your body, soul, and spirit with the things of God; His desires. Read and study the Word of God so that God can get down deep; to the very core of you to teach His ways of living life to glorify Himself! Pray out your deep conviction; tears streaming down your face like a waterfall or shouting at the top of your lungs; Father God doesn't care, just speak to Him from your heart! Boldly and confidently, but with humility talk to Father God because you and everything will be judged. Show mercy, love kindly, and walk humbly with your God! Help out others! Have faith in Lord Jesus Christ and stay strong in your faith to enter God's rest in life!

Chapter By Chapter

Chapter 5 Jesus Christ prayed prayers and prayed for what He wanted, but also, what He needed. Jesus shouted and cried when He prayed so we can too. Jesus became human so He can help us when we are being tempted or ignorant because He knows what we are going through. We learn best in our trials how to fully respect, trust, and cling to or rely on God the Father, Christ the Son, and the Holy Spirit through obedient submission. It's time to stand up and put your faith in Lord Jesus Christ into action in your life instead of being dependent on others. Rely on Father God to mold and mature you as well as your faith so that you know good from evil.

Chapter 6 Your faith cannot and should not stay at the level of knowing that you are saved through Jesus Christ; or thinking nonsense traditions are your ticket into Heaven. Through His Holy Spirit, Father God wants you to move forward in your faith of Lord Jesus Christ, in which you pray for people by laying on of hands, lend a helping hand, forgive, and continuing to love people. You need to be determined and have diligence in acting out your faith in Christ Jesus to prove that Father God is real and great is His love! Hook your hope in Jesus because He will not fail you if you are anchored to Him and know that His promises are true!

Chapter 7 You do not know how blessed you are when you allow Father God to use you. Sure you give your time, money, energy, and love. In return, God blesses you with blessings and teachings, in which you will cherish. Jesus is your high priest and is The Way to get to Father God. Jesus prepares and prevents or alters things on your behalf because that's how much He cares and loves you! Don't follow man-made rules about religion because the result is death. If you love Jesus, follow and obey His commandments found in the New Testament of the Bible.

Chapter 8 Sometimes too many rules are hindrances, in which people cannot live up to them or their heart is not sincere in performing the act behind the rule. Jesus Christ's ministry and His characteristics are what you should be striving to do and to be in life. God wants your heart and faith to be fully dependent on Him, in which you would go through fire for Him; believing and knowing that God is able to save you! Trust God because Jesus' death blessed you with better promises in life. Give Him your whole heart and life because He will strengthen your faith, in which the Bible will be on your mind and in your heart! Speak out and live out the Word of God to help Jesus change lives for God's glory! Remember the law of the old covenant is gone and is no more!

Chapter 9 Blood, Jesus Christ's blood makes whoever believes and calls upon the Name of the Lord Jesus Christ shall be saved; has right standing with God, is holy, blameless, and is forgiven. Jesus cleansed us from our sins and we have the privilege of serving the living God! If your heart, soul, mind, strength, and life are completely devoted to serving and honoring Father God, Jesus will speak to Father God on your behalf to see if He thinks you are ready for something. Jesus died once for all so religious traditions are useless. You will be judged, yet decide to live life honoring Father God on earth so you can know everlasting love and enter God's kingdom!

Chapter 10 Offerings, sacrifices, and religious traditions are pointless and are not what God desires. What Father God desires is for His children to strive for doing His will; saying and having full confidence in your faith in the Deity of the Godhead; Father, Son, and Holy Spirit. Don't let your faith be like a fishing bobber or a light that's on one minute, but in the next minute is off. Always be ready to share the gospel, how Father God transformed your life, and encourage others with the hope that's found in your everlasting God! Sharing your faith you will face opposition and persecution, but learning how to stay strong and firm in your faith from seeing fellow brothers and sisters in Christ matures your faith journey. Don't throw in the towel on God just because life is hard. Fight in prayer and allow God to fight for you! Put your faith, hope, and trust in God; keeping on doing His will for your life to receive His promises!

Chapter 11 "Now faith is confidence in what we hope for and assurance [certainty] about what we do not see." (Hebrews 11:1) "And without faith it is impossible to please God, because anyone who comes to him must believe that he exists and that he rewards those who earnestly seek him." (Hebrews 11:6) You have to have total confidence in your Lord to be unshaken when problems arise because this life on earth is your temporary home. If you believe in God, your home is in Heaven; Jesus is preparing it for you! Trust God and rely on His Holy Spirit in life because things can make us afraid or have questions; all you need to do is stand firm in your faith! Don't doubt God!

Chapter 12 It's easy to get wrapped up in sin and allow sin to hinder us from fixing our eyes on Jesus; focusing on all of the things that He has done for us; dying a horrendous death on the cross. He faced opposition, persecution, and suffered to be our perfect example for enduring hardships in our lives. In life, we face exciting and thrilling moments along with very hopeless moments. Look at the hopeless moments if you love God tremendously, with all that you are, view them as God is disciplining and training you for your next faith journey adventure with His Holy Spirit. Remember, "no discipline seems pleasant at the time, but painful. Later on, however, it produces a harvest of righteousness and peace for those who have been trained by it." (Hebrews 12:11) Live at peace; always loving and encouraging others. Speak out the truth of the gospel; always worship God in the highest respectable fear and in awe because you are so in love with Him! He can never be shaken as your Rock of your salvation!

Chapter 13 We need to put ourselves out there; being vulnerable in which we are loving, kind, will go the-extra-mile to help, and encouraging others. Act like this to strangers because you never know what Father God has in store or the good fruit/blessing that will come from it by acting out Christ's compassion on others. Try to put yourself in their shoes to experience the emotions that they are facing whether that would be pain, rejection, loss, brokenness, mistreated, or unfairness. Imagine you were in prison yourself and your emotions having to live there. God gives the final word, but allows Jesus to judge the nations, everyone, on the good and bad things we have done on earth. Seek God with all of your heart; chase Him, go after Him to intimately know God; having a close and strong relationship with Him, in which you absolutely without a doubt know that God satisfies your every longing. With this type of close fellowship with God, you can be content in every season, in which God has you in because if you ask for the Holy Spirit to live inside you, God is with you always; leading, guiding, and providing for you! So constantly praise Him, thank Him for all that He has done, share His gospel and your testimony with others unashamed, and do good deeds for the glory of God! He will equip you through His

Holy Spirit to fulfill His plan and purpose, just be obedient to Him!

End of <u>Hebrews</u>

Chapter By Chapter

James

Chapter 1 Don't allow your faith to waver or diminish in your trials. Your faith needs to be unwavering despite your difficulties because when you act out God's will, God is maturing and completing you; you will not be lacking anything. Don't have doubt in your entire body when you are praying to God because He wants to bless you abundantly beyond your abilities to think, hope, and ask for! Try not to waver or live according to what your selfish and self-centered body wants; striving for emptiness. Aim toward loving, serving God, and look after the orphans and widows. "My dear brothers and sisters, take note of this: Everyone should be quick to listen, slow to speak and slow to become angry, because human anger does not produce the righteousness that God desires. Therefore, get rid of all moral filth and the evil that is so prevalent and humbly accept the word planted in you, which can save you. Do not merely listen to the word, and so deceive yourselves. Do what it says." (James 1:19-22)

Chapter 2 Break out of your comfort zone; forget about the world's approve status quote and begin to lavish God's love, mercy, grace, and truth on everyone. Pray with and for them. Look for and spend time with someone who seems melancholy or who you think who doesn't seem to have much interaction in life. You should strive to get and stay involved with his or her life. Display through your actions what it means to be rightly living for God and rightly standing before God. Don't just say you have faith because you are just another fool; acting like many people on this earth. Love and acting in obedience to the Word (Bible) display your active intimate relationship with God!

Chapter 3 We need to come to the realization of how the words that we speak are deadly important. Positive thinking brings forth positive words; brings forth encouragement. If you continue to praise your Lord Jesus Christ, think on heavenly and trustworthy things, you will be joyful and be inspired to complete God's will in your life. Don't be a person who is a stop and goer, stop and goer, and stop and goer who speaks praises then curses out of the mouth. Choose who you want to be and stay consistent. Don't be bitter, envious or selfish. Don't boast about yourself. Seek God and His wisdom. "But the wisdom that comes from heaven is first of all pure; then peace-loving, considerate, submissive, full of mercy and good fruit, impartial and sincere." (James 3:17) Seek God to have these attributes!

Chapter 4 What are your motives when you are praying? Maybe you have the wrong motives and don't live your life honoring God. Evaluate your priorities and your pleasures; you may need to change them. God is not mocked. If you seriously want to know God, be done with evil schemes of the devil and submit to God's will and authority. He will reveal Himself to you the more you desire to know Him. God will fight your battles, but you have to humbly submit to His ways of living life. Often the word "lifetime" is pictured to be a long period of time, but it really isn't. Life is gone in an instant, a blink of an eye. You should be striving to help God to help people know Him. Speak about God to people and do good deeds because you honor God with your life! If you don't, you are living in sin and will have regrets.

Chapter 5 Wealth is depicted as happiness because you are free to buy pretty much anything. If you don't pay your expenses, you have many trials and are lonely. We, who are not extremely wealthy, still face trials of our own and choose to handle circumstances differently. Some will complain and hold grudges and be judgmental, but being an authentic, genuine follower of Jesus Christ, you know praying and asking God for help then implementing what He says to do or not to do sets you free from bondage. Remember Lord Jesus Christ is the only One who can and will judge everyone. Be someone who won't allow his or her faith to crumble and disappear under pressure from sufferings. Pray for patience and strength to persevere. Be someone who is loyal; keeping your word and displaying it in your actions. Keep everything simple. If you are rightly standing and rightly living for God, you have the privilege of praying to Father God and Him hearing your prayers in whatever fashion they come from your lips! Praying is powerful and effective so to defeat the devil and evil schemes, bondages, and chains, pray to God Most High about your cares. You should ask someone to pray for and with you so that you can be released from traveling down the wrong path; leading to death and destruction.

End of James

1 Peter

Chapter 1 God has given us His great love, mercy, and Holy Spirit. Life can bring us down because of the trials. We have to focus on our eternal hope in Christ Jesus and our inheritance, in which Jesus is preparing for us that last forever! We should strive to explain how intimacy with God, Jesus, and Holy Spirit is extremely important to fill us with His joy, peace, and kindness even though we cannot physically see Him. Share the knowledge and wisdom that Holy Spirit has blessed you with, with others because you desire for them to know Jesus! Your temporary home and life are here on earth so spread God's compassion around to others. Let your faith and hope that are in God arise!

Chapter 2 Don't let bitterness, anger, jealousy, rage, or resentment be tucked away super tight in your heart; blocking your intimacy with your Lord and with people. Relationships are different so don't compare others' relationships to yours. Father God just wants you to decide and desire what He wants, having a loving and intimate relationship; being completely obedient to His ways and timetable. Show compassion and forgiveness to others even when you totally and completely don't want to. Jesus Christ suffered, beaten, mocked, and was falsely accused; yet He endured it all to be your perfect example on the way of living life that glorifies and honors God! Be obedient onto the Lord in every situation!

Chapter 3 Honoring God in how He wants you to live, in respects to Him, has more worth than gold. When you decide to and are determined to act like Jesus as He tells you in His Word through His commandments, you will impact the kingdom of God for His glory and majesty! Continue to be steady in your faith in your Lord Jesus Christ; respecting and obeying authorities, praying, loving and nurturing people, doing what's right even when you know it will not be acceptable in the sight of men. Don't do paybacks with evil, but bless others with good deeds. Always be ready at any given moment to share your faith in Lord Jesus with others!

Chapter 4 You have to decide how to live your life; will you act in accordance to the truth of the gospel or settle to act like others act; repaying evil with evil? Study and read the Word to know how God expects you to live in accordance to His perfect will. Love with God's unfailing and unconditional love; sharing with each other life's struggles and joys. Serve out of your heart; loving your awesome Creator and Majesty! Remember suffering and being persecuted for Christ is a joy and tests your faith so don't be alarmed, but withstand your ground by continuing to do good deeds!

Chapter 5 Don't make others feel as if they are being a burden. You should always be more than willing to help in teaching God's ways and praying for others. Obey your authorities; be alert, and strive to be the best child of God that you know how to be. Push aside evil and ask God for help. Don't be stuck-up; try to learn from all situations and be humble; loving and doing good to everyone. Be God's child who holds onto and stands firm in your faith despite the trials and sufferings! If you stand firm, God will complete you in making you who you ought to be, His child. So share the gospel of Lord Jesus Christ; encouraging others to know Him intimately. Always be ready to testify and explain your faith in Christ Jesus to others!

End of 1 Peter

Chapter By Chapter

2 Peter

Chapter 1 You should choose to believe in Lord Jesus Christ and receive God's Holy Spirit to pray the perfect will of God and to know Him intimately. Holy Spirit will guide and teach you all things, the knowledge of God. When you don't have any doubt in your heart and truly believe in Jesus Christ, God blesses you with knowledge and the ability to live life that glorifies and honors Him. Act out your faith when you display goodness, the knowledge of God, self-control, perseverance, godliness, mutual affection, and love. God equips you to be able to act and be this type of person by you surrendering all control to Him. When you rely on Him, you don't live in your past sins, wrongdoings, or behaviors. Christ sets you free from all of that so you can be and act like Him; choosing to act out His calling and purpose for your life, choosing to shine His light and have His kingdom come down! Remember your life and body are shadows of the things to come. So make every effort to honor God in life!

Chapter 2 There are people who twist God's truth, Bible to be acceptable to what others want to hear. People will cloud and make the Word and Jesus' Name less powerful; accepting what God says not to do! You aren't rightly standing and rightly living with God on your own abilities; you are and have this because of Jesus Christ. He gives you His power to not live wickedly and turn away from evil destruction. Pour out your heart in prayer to God to ask Him for help to stop living deceitfully. Never stop believing in God, Jesus, and Holy Spirit or acting in firm faith because if you stop, you will pay bad consequences!

Chapter 3 When a change happens, you must repetitively implement it in your life to train yourself how to act. You should read and study the Word, Bible to get God's teaching down in your heart! Share God's gospel, teaching, and wisdom with others because God is a gentleman; He is waiting patiently for people to repent, turn away from their sin and fully rely on Him to have His way. Soon, very soon Jesus is coming on earth to make everything perfect. Be busy in displaying <u>the one true God</u> to people; share the grace and knowledge of Lord Jesus Christ with a wholesome mind!

End of <u>2 Peter</u>

Chapter By Chapter

<u>1 John</u>

Chapter 1 You should be bold and confident when you proclaim about Father God, Jesus Christ, and Holy Spirit with others. Testify about who your Lord is and all of what He has done for you. Speak the reasons for your hope, joy, peace, and love are in God Almighty at any given moment. Explain your actions if others question you about them because they notice that you are acting differently from everybody else. Jesus is the Light of the world and no darkness is in Him. He wants to take care of you, but you must turn away from evil and dark desires because light and darkness are not friends. Read the Bible and pray to God for desiring to be like Jesus!

Chapter 2 Come on, don't say one thing and do the other. Through the power of the Holy Spirit, God teaches and molds you on how to act like Jesus. You must listen and obey. Daily read the Bible, pray to God, listen to praise/worship songs, and fellowship with other believers. Everyday you are faced with decisions on how to act; loving, forgiving, and merciful, or mean, demanding, and selfish. If you are living for Christ, you know how to act that's pleasing to Him. Stop letting the actions of the world crowd or snuff out Jesus' light that's in you. So everyday read the Bible, pray to God, and listen to praise/worship songs to intimately know Him as well as His ways of living. Remaining in Him is nothing worth more than living life that glorifies Father God because nothing else matters!

Chapter 3 God, in His great ginormous love for us, His children, sent His Son Jesus Christ to die to make a way for us to freely rely upon Him. Knowing and actually walking in obedience to Jesus Christ cleanses us from our sins. One day soon, we will be fully and completely pure like Jesus is when we see Him face-to-face. When we know Father God intimately by reading Scripture and praying to Him continually, we are changed and molded into His image if we allow God by His Holy Spirit to transform us. Express God's love to others in actions of sincerity rather than just words. Love because not forgiving, hatred, and resentment destroy relationships. Act how you know Jesus wants you to act; if you feel condemned, change your behavior. If you are not condemned, you are confidently living for God! Obey Holy Spirit's guidance to live for God; obeying His commands and loving others!

Chapter 4 Through Holy Spirit, God teaches you, His child, if you sincerely believe in Him, how to tests prophecies and situations seeing if they are from God or not. If prophecies acknowledge Jesus than it's from God. If you don't have peace concerning certain situations, don't go forth and complete an action pertaining to that situation. God desires you to love, forgive, and show mercy to others. This is easier said than done especially when showing love, forgiveness, and mercy to family. Desire God to help you to act this way; relying on Him so that He can teach you to love others that's made perfect through knowing Him. Fear does not mix with love because perfect love drives out fear. If you are madly in love with God, lavish His kind of love and compassion on others so that you are not a hypocrite: saying you know Jesus and yet not acting like Him!

Chapter 5 Believing in Jesus Christ, you are God's child. If you truly are in love with God, you will obey His commands. They are not burdensome and through His Holy Spirit, God equips you with all that you need to overcome this evil world such as, the nine fruits of the Spirit, the nine gifts of the Spirit, and the armor of God. If you wholeheartedly believe in Jesus, you have eternal life. You have confidence in knowing and loving Him so you know that Father God hears your prayers and blesses you according to His will. God keeps you safe if you choose to be His child! As you seriously continue to know God intimately in building your relationship with Him, God will give understanding of Himself, the <u>one true God</u> and eternal life to you!

End of <u>1 John</u>

2 John

Chapter 1 Loving God, Jesus, and the Holy Spirit means that you desire to be like Jesus to everyone. You should be acting in patience, mercy, compassion, goodness, kindness, etc. Trials are like tests in building and maturing your faith. You can desire to go on your own and live by your standards, in which you stumble around. You can trust God; relying on Him to complete His plan in your life; patiently waiting for God to mold you in His unconditional love! Don't wish away seasons in your life; embrace, enjoy, and learn from them. Constantly act like Jesus no matter what; walking in the truth and love! Fight the good fight of faith and don't lose sight of Jesus!

End of 2 John

3 John

Chapter 1 Life is difficult and everything is fighting against you if you are truly a child of God. Read, study the Bible, and pray to Father God continually to allow your Lord and Savior to mold you. Transforming you from the inside out so you are walking in the truth. When you fix your eyes on Jesus, acting like Him, your life and health will be blessed! There are times when your faith is tested, in which you want to speak and act evil instead of showing hospitality to others. If you are in love with Jesus, you know what He would do so act it out! Persecution for Jesus is a joy and God will bless you according to your faith in Jesus! Walk in the truth until you see Jesus face-to-face so He can provide for you all day long!

End of 3 John

Jude

Chapter 1 Even though salvation in Jesus Christ is deathly, extremely important and you should be striving to help others to believe in Jesus Christ then living by faith in this world, the other most important quest is to never ever stop walking out your faith! You will have trials, opposition, and be faced persecution when you decide to be rightly standing and rightly living for God when you confidently know Him; are madly in love with Him! You can be mocked because of Jesus Christ, but you are freed from condemnation because all that you are is found in Jesus! Always love, forgive, and be merciful to others; praying in the Spirit to build yourself up in your most holy faith! Show fear, honor, and praise to God; explaining to others what it means to turn from sin to follow Jesus whose in control!

End of Jude

Revelation

Chapter 1 Often many people need to see something for them to believe it's real. The Word of God, (Bible,) Jesus' blood, and His testimony are your proof. You just have to believe and act in accordance to Him because Jesus is Truth! Patiently endure sufferings for Jesus and let His Spirit and characteristics overflow out of you to transform lives to increase the kingdom of Heaven. God created all good things and He has blessed us with Scripture as a double-edge sword. Go out and be a messenger for Jesus in this world!

Chapter 2 Even though God's children persevere, have tested prophecies, and don't participate with evil, if your heart isn't madly in love with Father God, Jesus Christ, and Holy Spirit, you have nothing because He desires your heart's devotion. Repent and turn toward God to begin a love relationship with Him again! God knows your afflictions, distress, poverty, bad reputation, and persecutions that you suffered; remain faithful to Lord Jesus Christ because He will greatly reward you. Though wickedness is prevalent more and more, you have to remain true to Jesus Christ and your faith in Him. Do everything for the glory of the Lord; in your actions, love, faith, service, and perseverance! Count everything as loss so that you don't try to see, hear, or understand with your natural functions. Believe in Jesus with all of your heart!

Chapter 3 You can be volunteering for ministries, helping children, giving donations, and visiting people, but if your heart isn't passionate for Christ, what you are doing is worthless. Nothing can separate you from the love of God; He is the One who opens and closes doors so God knows when you are wholeheartedly living and in love with Him or when you are halfheartedly, smidge, or completely not living for Him. Jesus knows when you are being persecuted for His Name and are patiently enduring it because Christ is your everything. You know that nothing in this earth satisfies your soul but Jesus. Go to Him for and about everything! You must be obedient to Holy Spirit when you are disciplined because God loves you immensely; He is maturing you so you can use everything He has properly! Sincerely, with your whole being, repent of wrongdoing so you can be fully victorious and unstoppable for Jesus Christ through His power! If you do, you will be richly rewarded!

Chapter 4 There is an opened door in Heaven. God, Jesus is sitting on His throne; encircling it is a rainbow with a sea of glass, clear as crystal, in front of His throne. Twenty-four thrones of twenty-four elders surround God's throne. In the center, but around the throne, there are four living creations, but I think they make up into one being. They along with the twenty-four elders worship, sing praises, give glory, and honor to Lord God Almighty continuously, day and night. You should worship, sing praises, give glory, and honor to Lord God Almighty all the daylong!

Chapter 5 Father God has a scroll that He wants open announces a mighty angel, but no one is worthy to open it. In walks in Jesus, the Lamb, who is slain to open the scroll. Jesus was beaten, spit at, mocked, scorn to make a way for every tribe, language, people, and nation to enter God's kingdom and to serve Him! Many, many, many angels, the four living creatures, and the twenty-four elders worship Jesus. But that's not all who is worshipping Jesus; every creature in Heaven, on earth, under the earth, on the sea, and everything will be worshipping Jesus! Worshipping your Lord and Creator doesn't need to be anything special or fancy. Just speak from your heart respecting God!

Chapter 6 The white horse and its' rider will bring forth God's rest, truth, humility, and justice on earth. A fiery red horse and its' rider will be sent out to take away peace and make people kill each other. A black horse and its' rider will, I think, cause people to become more blind and items will be expensive to purchase. A pale horse and its' rider, Death will be chasing the realm of the dead. Their power will cause people to be killed by sword, famine and plague, and by the wild beasts of the earth. Under the altar are the souls of God's children, your brothers and sisters in Christ Jesus who stood firm in their faith and were persecuted for Jesus Christ's sake. We will be given a white robe because of Christ's righteousness! We will have to wait for all of our brothers and sisters to suffer and be persecuted for Jesus Christ Name's sake. A great earthquake will occur. The sun will turn black. The moon will turn blood red and the stars up in the sky will fall upon the earth. The heavens receded like a scroll being rolled up, and every mountain and island was removed from its place. The world will be extremely chaotic; people will not know which way to turn. Death will seem like an escape from the wrath of God. Judgment Day is coming so be ready!

Chapter 7 Four angels will be given the power to cause no wind to blow on the earth. The land, sea, and trees will not be harmed until other angels put a seal on the foreheads of the servants of God. When the great tribulation and persecution are over, Father God's children will be dressed in white robes worshipping God with palm branches and their voices. Jesus, His death and resurrection, and His blood are what make us be right standing before God! Desire to serve God both day and night because He alone is the One who shelters you from harm! He provides for your every need if you are obedient to His voice. In Heaven, there are not tears!

Chapter 8 When Jesus, the Lamb opens the seventh seal, there is silence in Heaven for a half hour. Then seven angels stand before God while He hears the prayers of His children. When the prayer aroma is finished, the censer will be filled with fire and hurled down to earth causing destruction by severe weather elements. Seven angels will sound trumpets; three of which will cause the earth to be burned up in thirds, and a blazing fire mountain will destroy sea life; everything pertaining to the sea. A blazing great star will fall from the sky to cause a third of the rivers and springs to be bitter. This will cause people to die because of the bitterness. A third of the sun, moon, and stars will become darken. Also a third of the day and night will not shine forth their light. In mid-Heaven, a flying eagle will pronounce the ultimate shame on the rest of mankind because three more trumpets will be sounded. Chapter 9 I am a visual learner, so if possible, I like to see a picture to remember concepts better. On page 148 there are pictures of a scorpion, a locust, and what these insects may look like in the last days after the great star releases smoke from the bottomless pit, as if it were a gigantic furnace. People who don't worship, respect, or honor Father God will be tormented severely; making people want to die because of the torture. Certain four angels will be released to kill a third of mankind. Another third of mankind will be killed by not-your-average-kind-of-horses; power to inflict injury. After all of these events and dealings, people who don't die, won't repent or worship God Almighty; they worship idols and demons, etc. Chapter 10 A mighty angel is robed in a cloud, a rainbow is above his head, his face is like the sun, and his legs are fiery pillars comes down from Heaven. He holds an opened little scroll straddling the sea and land of the earth with his feet. He will shout something when this great day comes; it will sound like a roar of a lion and the voices of the seven thunders will speak. It's a mystery what they say. When the seventh angel is about to sound his trumpet that is when the mystery of God will be accomplished. We may understand the fullness of God and His will completely and totally perfect; with no flaw bodies limiting us. Right now, our job or mission is to share the gospel of Lord Jesus Christ with everyone on earth and act like Jesus! Don't let your fiery passion for God be bottled up inside of you because that will be harmful. Prophecy, a word from God, can strengthen, encourage, or bring correction for someone so speak the word and the gospel of Lord Jesus Christ!

Chapter 11 Two witnesses will prophesy for three and one-half years in the Holy City. If anyone tries to harm them, fire will come out of their mouths and they have the power to kill people. The two witnesses will have the power to cause no rain to come upon the earth and to send down every kind of plague as often as they want. When they are finished with their testimony about God, Jesus, Holy Spirit, the beast will overpower and kill them. They won't be buried. People will celebrate because the two witnesses or prophets tormented people who live on the earth. After three and a half days, God will give the two witnesses the breath of life to terrorize people when they are seen. When a loud voice says, "Come up here." the two witnesses will go to Heaven in a cloud and their enemies will gaze upon them. The seventh trumpet will be sounded by an angel and in Heaven, loud voices will exclaim praises to Lord God Almighty. The twenty-four elders, who are seated on their thrones before God, will fall down on their faces and will worship God. God's temple in Heaven will open and the ark of His covenant is seen. Different weather patterns will rage.

Chapter 12 Think of Jesus' birth; Herod commanded that every male child from two-years-old and younger to be killed. I think that the woman symbolizes Mary giving birth to Jesus and Satan trying to kill, steal, and destroy God's kingdom with his evil schemes. A lesson that can be implied here is when your life feels as though it's spinning out of control and you are scared, God will come through for you; He has a plan and is making a way for your well-being and safety. Satan and his angels will be hurled down on earth. A loud voice in Heaven will proclaim praises to Jesus and exclaim victory over Satan by the blood of the Lamb and the word of our testimony! Satan knows his time is short to destroy people's lives and make them avoid following God's commands as well as their testimony about Jesus. Chaos, temptations will I think, be even greater and significant in the last days of the last days. God will do something magnificent to save you from the clutches of Satan, but God knows what He will do in this final hour.

Chapter 13 The first beast will come out of the sea who will be disrespectful of God and give a negative reputation of the Lord's people. People will be filled with wonder and will worship the beast. It will be given power to rage war against God's holy people and to overcome them. He has authority over every tribe, people, language, and nation. Whoever's names are not written in the Lamb's book of life will be subject to be killed by going into captivity or by a sword. God's people will have to have patient endurance as well as faithfulness as people come into the end of time. There's a second beast that will perform great signs, even causing fire to come down from Heaven to the earth in full view of the people. The second beast will deceive people of the earth with performing great signs. People will be ordered to set up an image in honor of the beast that was wounded by the sword and yet lived. Everyone; great and small, rich and poor, free and slave, will have to receive a mark on their right hands or on their foreheads, so that they cannot buy or sell unless they have the mark, which is the name of the beast or the number of its name. Evil is raging so prepare for battle by reading and actively living out God's Word, Bible!

Chapter 14 On Mount Zion will stand Jesus, the Lamb along with His 144,000 children who have His Name and His Father's

Name on their foreheads. Before God's throne and before the four living creatures and the elders, a harp, a roar of rushing waters, and a peal of thunder will be the melody and chords of the new song sing by only God's 144,000 children. They will be the only ones who know the song because they remained virgins, follow Jesus wherever He goes, remained faithful to Jesus because He died on the cross for them, and no lies are on their lips so they are blameless. The first angel will be flying in midair proclaiming the good news of the gospel to people who live on the earth-to every nation, tribe, language, and people. With a loud voice, he will proclaim glory and praise to God! The second angel will make all of the nations receive revenge because of their rebellious ways. The third angel will send forth God's wrath in full strength because people worship the beast and its image. No rest for these people and they will be tormented in front of the holy angels and of the Lamb. Again God's children need to have patient endurance and keep God's commands while remaining faithful to Christ! Live and die for your Lord because you will be richly rewarded. Jesus and His angels will harvest the earth; separating the followers of Christ from the unbelievers.

Chapter 15 A great and marvelous sign in Heaven will be seven angels with seven trumpets to complete God's wrath which will be the seven of the last plagues. People who are victorious in not worshipping the beast, its image, and decide not to receive the number/name will be standing beside the fiery glass sea. God will give harps to them and they will sing the song of Moses and of the Lamb. The tabernacle of the covenant law in the temple in Heaven is opened. The seven angels with seven trumpets to complete God's wrath will be dressed in clean, shining linen, and golden sashes around their chests. They will be given seven golden bowls to fill them with God's wrath. The temple will be filled with God's glory and power, and no one can enter the temple until the seven plagues of the seven angels are completed.

Chapter 16 From the temple in Heaven, a loud voice will command the seven angels to perform their duties. Ugly, feasting sores will break out on the people who worship the beast and its image. The sea will turn into blood and it will make every living thing in the sea die. The rivers and springs of water will turn into blood by the third angel. The angel in charge of the rivers and springs will proclaim praises to Lord God Almighty. The sun will be allowed to scorch people with fire and yet with the intense heat people still won't repent or glorify God. The beast and its kingdom will be plunged into darkness. People will gnawed their tongues in agony and will curse the God of Heaven, but they will refuse to repent of what they have done. The great river of Euphrates will be dried up so that kings can battle against impure spirits, dragons, the beast, and false prophets. Lastly, the seventh angel pours his bowl into the air and a loud voice from the throne will say, "It is done!" Flashes of lightning, rumblings, peals of thunder, and a severe earthquake will occur. The great city will be split into three parts. Every island and mountain will flee. Huge hailstones will fall on the people making them decide to curse God because of the hail plague.

Chapter 17 A woman will be sitting on the beast and she will be punished for prostitution, adulteries, and other abominable things; covered in disrespectful names concerning God. Disgrace will come to her. The woman, the beast, and kings will rage war against the Lamb, but the Lamb will triumph over them because he is Lord of Lords and King of Kings—and with him will be his called, chosen and faithful followers. Read verses 17 and 18 again. Pray to God for understanding and clarity about this chapter because I'm confused myself. I don't know how to help you. Sorry!

Chapter 18 Babylon, the great city will receive Lord God Almighty's wrath because she led the people astray. She bought all of their merchandise to supply them with wealth. God will judge her with judgments that she so deserves and everyone will turn their backs on her!

Chapter 19 The great multitude in Heaven will shout praises to God who sits on His throne. The four living creatures and the twenty-four elders will shout praises to God. A roar of rushing waters and loud peals of thunder come along with the great multitude of people shouting praises to God. All of God's children who desire to know Lord God Almighty, love Him, and are in love with Him will finally celebrate and enjoy the webbing banquet of the Lamb. Worship God Almighty because you know without a doubt that the testimony of Jesus is true! Jesus Christ, Faithful and True will be riding a white horse defeats the beast! The beast and the false prophet will be captured; thrown alive into the fiery lake of burning sulfur. The kings of the earth and their armies will be killed with the sword coming out of the mouth of the rider on the white horse, and all the birds will gorged themselves on their flesh.

Chapter 20 An angel will come down from Heaven to seize and bind up Satan to stop him from deceiving the nations for a thousand years with the key to the bottomless pit and a great chain. God's children and their souls who do not worship the beast and its image, don't receive the mark of the beast because they kept the faith in Jesus Christ, His testimony, and in the Word of God will rule and reign over nations with Christ for a thousand years. When the thousand years are over, Satan will be released again to deceive the nations; surrounding God's holy people and the city He loves. Fire will be thrown from Heaven to devour people who choose to believe Satan's lies. Along with Satan, they will be thrown into the lake of burning sulfur, where the beast and the false prophet had been thrown. They will be tormented day and night for ever and ever. Then Jesus who sits on His great white throne will judge people, great and small with the books opened. The Book Of Life will be opened as well. The dead will be judged according to what they have done as recorded in the books. Anyone whose name is not found written in the Book Of Life will be thrown into the Lake of Fire. The Lake of Fire is the second death.

Chapter 21 Now, those people whose names are written in the Lamb's Book Of Life and are victorious in testifying about Jesus Christ will be united with God Almighty! The anticipation of God waiting for His bride, the Church and the Church dressed beautifully waiting for her Husband will be over! God will create a new Heaven and a new Earth, in which there will be no more death, mourning, crying, pain, for the old order of things has passed away. He will wipe every tear from their eyes. God will make everything new! "Those who are victorious will inherit all this, and I will be their God and they will be my children. But the cowardly, the unbelieving, the vile, the murderers, the sexually immoral, those who practice magic arts, the idolaters and all liars—they will be consigned to the fiery lake of burning sulfur. This is the second death." (Revelation 21:7-8) The New Jerusalem will be glorious and marvelous; far above what we can hope, think, and imagine! Nothing impure will ever enter it, nor will anyone who does what is shameful or deceitful....

Chapter 22 The river of the water of life is clear as crystal flows from the throne of God and of the Lamb. Each side of the river stands the tree of life yielding its fruit every month. And the leaves of the tree are for the healing of the nations. No longer will there be any curse. The throne of God and of the Lamb will be in the city, and His servants will serve Him. We, His children, His bride will see Jesus face-to-face and His Name will be on our foreheads! There will be no more night. They will not need the light of a lamp or the light of the sun, for the Lord God will give them light. And they will reign for ever and ever. The time is near when Jesus is coming back soon when everything is new; the time is nearer and closer everyday! "Let the one who does wrong continue to do wrong; let the vile person continue to be vile; let the one who does right continue to do right; and let the holy person continue to be holy." Read verses 14 and 15. Come to Jesus because He satisfies all your needs! Jesus is coming so be ready and continue how you choose to live. Eternal life or the Lake of Fire, live life how you want to because the choice is yours.

End of Revelation

Chapter By Chapter

 A scorpion

 A locust

 What scorpions and locusts may look like in the last days.

About The Author

"Neither this man nor his parents sinned," said Jesus, "but this happened so that the works of God might be displayed in him."

John 9:3

Emily Zondlak is in love with Christ and in an intimate relationship with Him! God is her number One in her life! God, her Father has blessed Emily so much with family, friends, and experiences in her life that no words can express! She chooses to follow Him on His path for her life because His plan is far better than she could have done if she chose to do it on her own! Emily is determined to do everything as God lays the task down.

Emily's Bible verse for her life is John 9:3. Many people think that handicapped people desire to live without their disability. This is not true for Emily! Her intimate relationship with God Almighty has molded her to be content in being physical disabled and nonverbal. She has had many people who assumed that she wanted to be healed from her disability and quoted Scripture verses of Jesus healing people. Also Emily has had people who prayed over her because she was not confident enough to say, "No, thank you." Sure she faces daily challenges more than other people and that does not bother her because her aim is on seeking God, knowing Him, and helping others know Him intimately. In life, circumstances unfolding will not make sense. People can step out in faith believing and trusting that God will do what He wants. Time is becoming shorter until the day that Jesus comes back on the earth. As children of God, everyone needs to be spreading the gospel. No one else can spread or act like Christ as certain individuals can. Others may not stand up for Jesus. God created each person unique! People have a purpose that God made for them and only they can fulfill.

Emily is on fire for the Lord Jesus Christ and wants to fragrance the world with Christ! Her anchor holds within the veil! With God's Holy Spirit's help, Emily has published Open H†S Word also. Emily hopes the intimacy with Jesus Christ will become stronger when reading the Bible, Open H†S Word, and Chap†er By Chap†er!

www.ingramcontent.com/pod-product-compliance
Lightning Source LLC
Chambersburg PA
CBHW071630080526
44588CB00010B/1350